"Dr. Godley has written a very readable and eminently practical guide to living a happier, more fulfilling and productive life. The book provides advice on becoming more nurturing of ourselves, living in the present, altering our internal dialogue when it is self-defeating, and understanding and recognizing life choices. Within these important categories, the book covers a broad scope of human problems. You will find ideas you probably have not encountered before, such as the 'tornado analogy' for coping with regret, the 'brick analogy' for helping you move in the direction of goals you have set for yourself, or the 'should closet' for handling unrealistic expectations of yourself. Numerous vignettes help bring the tools Dr. Godly describes into practical, ready-to-use advice that many readers will be able to identify with and benefit from.

"More than just a 'self-help' guide, *Four Principles for Facing Life's Challenges* reads like advice from a beloved teacher or nurturing mentor. Dr. Godley's sharing of her own challenges of coping with blindness is especially inspiring. The book illustrates how to gain a higher degree of control over your life. It is both comforting and inspiring. I dare say most readers will find plenty of useful tips and encouragement here to deal with everyday problems of stress, anxiety, or discouragement. Highly recommended."

Victor Ashear, Ph.D., author of *Self-Acceptance:*
*The Key to Recovery from Mental Illness*

"Dr. Godley's ability to capture and conceptualized thoughts and ideas and translate them into clear, concise written form, without losing the original intent and meaning, is a great talent. It makes her a dream to work with as a co-author, as does the unique combination of creativity, clarity, and passion she possesses."

Marc Gillard, co-author of "Assisting Handlers Following Attacks on Dog Guides: Implications for Dog Guide Teams," Guide Dogs for the Blind, San Rafael, CA

"I found Cheryl's book to be enlightening and a breath of fresh air. The book provides explanations about certain situations we all go through in life and describes that we all have choices. A lot of self-help books focus on what people have done wrong and how they should fix it. I didn't feel that way at all reading this book. There is no right or wrong—it is all a choice. I felt the book was written extremely well to reach readers in personalizing obstacles. The writer shows she is opening up and speaking from learning experiences, rather than talking at the reader. I would recommend this book to all."

Samantha Anderson, Office Manager of Adbay, Casper, WY

# Book and Author Endorsements

"I have known Dr. Cheryl Godley as both a psychologist and a friend for over 18 years. Dr. Godley is a highly competent and successful clinician. Her visual impairment has only served to sharpen her understanding of people. Dr. Godley has drawn from her decades of experience to create manageable, effective action plans that encourage and direct change. She offers practical, helpful solutions to the complexities of life's problems. This book is written for anyone seeking to lead a more satisfying life. Professionals will find it useful in therapy as well."

Julie L. Fox, M.S., L.P.C., Clinical Director of
The Healing Place, Casper, WY

"Dr. Godley is known for her ability to explain complex issues in a manner that is organized and easy to understand. She is dedicated to both the art and science of the craft, blending the scientific foundations of her study with taking time to learn how it applies to individual persons. This work is enlightening and beneficial."

Stephen J. Juergens, Executive Director of Wyoming
Services for Independent Living, Cody, WY

"The takeaway from one of Cheryl's presentations is the knowledge that you have been exposed to some very useful information that has been researched thoroughly. Her professional demeanor made it clear, in no uncertain terms, that she knew what she was talking about."

Tom Lealos, former President of the Wyoming Council of the Blind

"Dr. Godley is the most creative, innovative, and talented therapist I have encountered over the past 30-plus years of psychiatric practice. She is exceptional in her ability to assist others in dramatically improving the quality of their lives. Both mental health clinicians and the general public will enjoy reading Dr. Godley's book, *Four Principles for Facing Life's Challenges: A Guide for Making Choices that Build Life Satisfaction*. Relying on her many years of clinical experience as a psychologist, Dr. Godley has formulated a systematic approach to addressing life's day-to-day struggles. Her extensive psychological knowledge base is blended with self-reflection and appropriate sharing of her own personal history. Dr. Godley is a wise and empathic clinician. A wealth of clinical 'pearls' is presented in a very readable, warm, and engaging fashion. Clinicians will find the material very useful in their therapeutic endeavors. The general public will find that application of these principles will assist in continued personal growth."

Timothy B. Hudson, M.D., Diplomate of the American Board of Psychiatry and Neurology, Terre Haute, IN

"Dr. Godley has a wonderful conversational writing style that draws you in. This distillation of her years of clinical experience gives us all practical tools to reduce stress and bring greater joy to our lives. This book is a gem!"

Deborah A. Bronk, Ph.D., President and CEO, Bigelow Laboratory for Ocean Sciences, East Boothbay, ME

# Four Principles for
# Facing Life's Challenges

Four Principles for

# FACING LIFE'S CHALLENGES

## A Guide for Making Choices that Build Life Satisfaction

# CHERYL GODLEY, Ph.D.

the
Write
Place

PUBLISHING + DESIGN

Print book ISBN: 978-0-9994887-7-5
E-book ISBN: 978-1-7330085-0-1

Library of Congress Control Number: 2019940448

Published in the United States of America by the Write Place, Inc.
For more information, please contact:

the Write Place, Inc.
809 W. 8th Street, Suite 2
Pella, Iowa 50219
www.thewriteplace.biz

Cover and interior design by Michelle Stam, the Write Place, Inc.
Cover stock photo by Ajgul, shutterstock.com.

Copies of this book may be ordered online at cherylgodley.com, Amazon, and BarnesandNoble.com.

View other Write Place titles at www.thewriteplace.biz.

# THIS BOOK IS DEDICATED TO ALL SERVICE ANIMALS

I want to especially dedicate this book to my past guide dogs, Ynez, Jared, and Reece, my present guide dog, Diaz, and my future guide dogs. They have all been outstanding workers who have assisted me to live independently. Each had their own personality that set them apart and enriched my life. They have been loved companions who have reciprocated that love through loyalty and service. My guide dogs have been an integral part of my life.

## THIS BOOK IS DEDICATED TO ALL SERVICE ANIMALS

I want to especially dedicate this book to my past guide dogs, Ynez, Jared, and Reece, my present guide dog, Diaz, and my future guide dogs. They have all been outstanding workers who have assisted me to live independently. Each had their own personality that set them apart and enriched my life. They have been loved companions who have reciprocated that love through loyalty and service. My guide dogs have been an integral part of my life.

# CONTENTS

# PRINCIPLE IV
# Understanding and Recognizing Choices in Life

# CONCLUSION

# The Four Principles and Life Satisfaction

# FOREWORD

Psychologist Dr. Cheryl Godley's new book—*Four Principles for Facing Life's Challenges: A Guide for Making Choices that Build Life Satisfaction*—is a gem. Although based on sound psychological principles and science, she has managed to create a fun-to-read self-help book that will appeal to everyone. Her use of numerous interesting and enlightening stories to illustrate her points on how to live a more productive and fulfilling life will resonate with young and old alike. Readers will learn a number of ways to apply the ideas outlined in this book, which help effectively manage the difficulties and problems that occur in daily life. The concise steps to changing non-adaptive behavioral habits are clearly outlined in each chapter.

While there are many self-help books on the market, it is rare to find one that has such a universal appeal as this easy-to-read book. As a psychologist myself, I have often found self-help books to be limited in their scope and not engaging. Dr. Godley has blended her professional clinical experiences with sound psychological theory to provide useful suggestions for self-improvement in an entertaining and informative manner. I highly recommend her book for your reading enjoyment and better understanding of four basic principles to leading a more productive and happy life.

Charles Davidshofer, Ph.D., retired Associate Professor of Psychology and Director of the University Counseling Center, Colorado State University, Fort Collins, CO

# PREFACE

## The Purpose and Creation of This Book

I have always known I was going to write this book. It has been an idea that would not go away, no matter how busy I became or how much my vision declined, making writing more and more difficult. Somehow, some way, I would make *Four Principles for Facing Life's Challenges: A Guide for Making Choices that Build Life Satisfaction* a reality.

Also spurring me on was the question I often hear from clients: "When are you going to write a book?" They believe that what they are learning in therapy is life-changing. They want something concrete to refer to for themselves on their own, and they also want a way to share what they are learning with others. Many friends who are in the mental health profession and have read my rough drafts have also encouraged me to finish this book, so they may share it with their own clients.

Increasing insurance limitations are decreasing opportunities to engage in therapy. I am concerned that people have fewer opportunities to learn effective coping strategies. My hope is *Four Principles for Facing Life's Challenges* may provide basic skills for effectively living life to anyone seeking personal growth.

The information presented in this book is not treatment or therapy, and its purpose is not to be a substitute for professional therapy. However, *Four Principles for Facing Life's Challenges* may offer readers the opportunity for personal growth, for gaining personal insight and self-reflection, and for considering and learning different ways to approach life's challenges. If this information is used in conjunction with therapy, readers may experience more and richer benefit from the therapeutic process.

The beauty of *Four Principles for Facing Life's Challenges* is that it may be used as a guide to learning strategies for coping with life's challenges. It allows readers to proceed at their own pace, without the expectation of having to achieve particular goals within a certain timeframe. Some people may be looking for avenues of personal growth but are intimidated by the structure and perceived expectations that come from workshops or self-help groups. Because of the scope and near-universal applicability of the skills and strategies presented here, readers at almost any stage in their lives and experiencing a wide variety of stressors will benefit from this book.

I use the skills and strategies presented in *Four Principles for Facing Life's Challenges* on a daily basis as I cope with my own life's stress—in particular, stress resulting from vision loss. While I appreciate and cognitively understand how and why the Four Principles work on a professional level, they also continually touch and enrich my life on a personal level. The Four Principles work for me, no matter how much unexpected stress I encounter.

# Self-Introduction

At this point, it may be helpful to introduce a certain part of myself—my visual impairment. I am legally and functionally blind. I see movement, color contrast, and light. I do not see details of anything. I have some peripheral vision, but no central vision. If I look at something, it disappears. I travel with my fourth guide dog, Diaz.

Sweet Diaz is my "right paw." He is with me everywhere—in the office, on my travels, at the grocery store, at restaurants. He sleeps and snores and hogs my bed. He has even guided me through the streets of Paris.

I am writing this book through dictation to my computer, which has a screen reader that talks to me and tells me what is written on the screen. My computer can also produce either braille or print. I obviously do not drive, and you wouldn't want me to! I walk to work or use public transportation and drivers to get around. I cook. I clean, and I have a housekeeper who comes in every other week to assist. I try to keep my closet organized, but there are times when it is necessary to ask my husband to assist me to find things. A friend shops with me to make sure

I pick out appropriate clothes. Without her assistance, I may unknowingly dress like a rodeo clown.

Because of my visual limitations, even basic tasks may take a lot more time and a lot more energy than they would for the average person. I hope this description provides you with an idea of how I approach some of my life's tasks. While I perceive myself as Cheryl, it is necessary for me to approach things differently than most people. Understanding that I have visual limitations may help you understand the examples and illustrations I use throughout the book.

# Organization of the Book

Each of the Four Principles is divided into sections that provide skills and strategies to help you develop that principle. The psychological background each skill and strategy is rooted in is presented, along with analogies to assist in understanding the concepts. Each skill and strategy is explained in a step-by-step, easy-to-learn fashion. Self-reflection challenges are included at the end of each chapter to assist in assimilating, developing, and implementing the Four Principles. These opportunities for self-reflection are targeted to guide you in exploring and personalizing the skills and strategies in a way that best suits your unique circumstances.

The examples that demonstrate the coping strategies for each principle use fictitious characters and circumstances. They are not to be construed as actual individuals or events. The only exceptions are the examples I pull from my own life in coping with my loss of vision.

# Acknowledgments

I would like to thank clients who have shared their lives with me and entrusted me to join with them in their life's challenges and journeys. Their experiences have assisted in developing the Four Principles. I appreciate the hard work they have invested in themselves to make changes in their lives. They have taught me so much and have enriched my life.

I am extremely grateful to the friends, family, and colleagues who provided encouragement and support throughout the development of this book. They have stood by me throughout this project. They have also used their valuable time and energy to read drafts of the manuscript and provide helpful feedback. Each individual has had a unique impact on the book. Thank you to each of you.

I would like to express my gratitude to Jack McHugh, my literary consultant, for guiding me through each step of the publishing maze. At the Write Place, Sarah Purdy, my editor and publishing consultant, and Michelle Stam, my print and digital designer, have provided outstanding feedback and suggestions for the book. Their expertise has been invaluable in getting the manuscript into book form. Thank you for your assistance and for teaching me about the publishing process.

I have been blessed to know and to learn from many mentors throughout my training and professional life. I was fortunate to have had excellent clinical supervisors during my doctoral training who played a significant role in developing my skills as a clinician. Many of my instructors taught me the importance of continually evaluating and seeking out sound, empirical foundations in the field of psychology. Two individuals who have highly influenced me stand out.

Psychologist Dr. Charles Davidshofer, retired former Associate Professor of Psychology and Director of the University Counseling Center at Colorado State University, is one of the most outstanding professionals I know. His knowledge of psychological assessment is stellar and brilliant. He is an incredible, amazing resource. If I ever have a clinical question, I still talk and consult with him.

The other mentor who has provided invaluable lessons is psychologist Dr. Jerry Deffenbacher, retired former Professor of Psychology at Colorado State University, who served as the head of my dissertation committee. We spent many hours discussing theoretical orientations in the field of psychology. He challenged me to consider different perspectives and ways of approaching psychological concepts. He taught me how to process theoretical concepts from multiple dimensions and perspectives and assimilate them into a foundational framework that works for me as a psychologist. Even after many years, we periodically continue our discussions. I still find them personally and intellectually stimulating.

I feel honored and fortunate to have learned and continue to learn from both of these mentors. They are both much more than colleagues. They are outstanding models of all that is "psychological" in the field of psychology.

There is no way for me to express my gratitude to my office manager and friend of many years, Tom Smyth. When I told him I was working on this book, he graciously offered to help, so I might reduce the onerous visual drain associated with writing. He wanted to free me up so I might focus on the creative aspects and not have to worry about ensuring the print was where it was supposed to be. Tom and I have spent many hours together each week, combing through and reworking what I have written. I have appreciated his feedback, ideas, and contributions.

Our process was extremely creative, bouncing ideas back and forth—some of which became fun and silly, devolving into free association and lots of laughter. At other times, the process was grueling, as we racked our brains for just the right way to present an idea or concept. During those times, when I was intensely focused, Tom had a way of using his wit, banter, and unpredictable responses to break through my concentration and bring laughter and a fresh perspective. Without Tom, this project would not be what it is. He has spared me the visual agony of the editing process. I have also appreciated his never-ending professional and personal support, both in writing this book and over the years in my clinical practice.

I want to thank psychologist Dr. Susan MacQuiddy, retired Director of Counseling Services at Colorado State University

Health Network. She first introduced me to the work of Dr. Irvin Yalom during a course in existential theory in psychology that I took during my doctoral studies. It was one of my favorite classes; I remember pouring myself into the course literature, spending hours thinking through and about the proponents of existential theory. While Dr. Yalom's profound work has presented foundational approaches in group psychotherapy, he is also known for his work in writing about existential theory and for his prolific novel writing.

The information in his book *Existential Psychotherapy* (1980)—where he presents his psychodynamic theory—became the focus of my doctoral dissertation. Dr. Yalom's psychodynamic theory is summarized in Appendix A for those who are interested in learning about it. My dissertation research looked at the variables Dr. Yalom presents in his theory and tested the relationships between them. A summary of the research findings from my doctoral dissertation on the relationships between death anxiety, locus of control, and life satisfaction is provided in Appendix B.

The existential perspective is highly theoretical. When Dr. Yalom presented the concept of locus of control as a means to measure defensive styles for coping, I perceived it as significant because it provided a means to grasp and quantify a part of the theory. The idea of locus of control serving as a construct to evaluate how an individual lives their life was the seed that grew over my years of clinical practice and personal experience. This seed of an idea bloomed into a primary construct underlying the development of the Four Principles for building life satisfaction. The Four Principles are:

Principle I: Self-nurturing and taking care of myself

Principle II: Living in the present

Principle III: Developing a positive relationship with myself

Principle IV: Understanding and recognizing choices in life

When I read the work of Dr. Yalom, it resonated with ideas I had identified in facing my life experiences. In particular, it related to my loss of vision. Facing that I had lost—and was continuing to lose—my vision had already led me to believe that living life is a choice and that it is within our choice to decide how well we live life.

Purists of different theoretical orientations—whether it be behavioral, cognitive, existential, humanistic, and so on— may scoff at my mixing of genres of theoretical orientation in the skills and strategies I present in the Four Principles. While I respect the perspective of purists, when it comes to living, in my mind it is down to learning to make choices that lead to an effective and efficient life. If that means applying skills identified in the literature as effective for coping, but that also cross the line into other theoretical orientations, then so be it.

The coping strategies selected to support each principle in this book come from established work in different theoretical orientations in psychology. For example, the concepts that underlie the importance of staying in the present come from mindfulness-based cognitive therapy literature and may include the work of individuals like Jon Kabat-Zinn, who is noted for his work in mindfulness-based stress reduction. The concepts that underlie the importance of internal dialogue come from literature in the cognitive-behavioral theoretical orientation and includes work of individuals like Martin Seligman, who is noted for his work in positive psychology. The concept of vicarious learning, or model learning, comes from Albert Bandura's social learning theory. Similarly, ideas related to the child analogy of internal dialogue draw upon the work of Eric Berne in his concepts presented in transactional analysis. Noting the importance of recognizing choices and consequences comes out of John Broadus Watson and Edward Thorndike's foundational work in behavioral psychology. This idea was further developed by B. F. Skinner in operant conditioning, and it may also be perceived as coming out of a foundational principle in existential psychology that states that we all have our own choices in life and that each choice has a consequence. Thus, the coping strategies presented are grounded in psychological literature and may draw upon a variety of theoretical orientations and the work of individuals within those orientations. My primary focus is to assist people in learning how to live fuller, richer lives. My hope is that this book provides helpful and meaningful information and that readers choose to apply the skills and strategies I present to attain the Four Principles that build life satisfaction.

It goes without saying that I want to thank my husband, Gary, for his support and belief in me. My vision had begun to deteriorate before we met. He easily accepted the world of visual impairment into his own life, and it is second nature to him. For instance, he automatically describes what he is seeing as we travel. It is quite amusing that he catches himself describing things to sighted people and has to remind himself it is not necessary. I most appreciate that he does not define me in any other way, except that I am Cheryl. I told him many years ago when we first married that I intended to write a book. He never let me forget this dream. Now, the first book is done. Other books will follow, and they will adhere to the conviction that life is made up of choices. Regardless of our circumstances, we are all capable of improving our lives.

# CHAPTER 1

---

# Setting the Stage and Understanding the Theory

## Introduction

### A NEW DAY

Is this you?

The alarm clock goes off at 4:00 a.m. I set it for 4:00 a.m. because I wanted to work out. But I'm too tired. I turn off the alarm and reset it for 5:00 a.m. I hope an extra hour of sleep will give me more energy to get all the stuff done that I need to get done. Rather than falling back to sleep, I lie in bed mulling over all of the things I have to do today.

The hour passes without a wink of sleep. The alarm goes off again—5:00 a.m. I jump out of bed, use the restroom, run to the kitchen, and turn on the coffee. I gulp down breakfast. I grab my coffee and scurry to jump in the shower. I get dressed and throw my things together for work.

*Don't forget those papers.*

*I've got to pick up that prescription.*

*I've got to be prepared for that big meeting today.*

As I'm thinking through my day, I realize the kids are up. One is telling me they can't find their sock, the other is upset their sister isn't getting out of the bathroom quickly enough, and another is still in bed. I take care of the perceived catastrophes. I sprint back down to the kitchen, grab the cereal and the milk, and flop it on the table along with bowls and spoons.

After much commotion, I finally drop the kids off at school. I'm running late. Heavy on the gas, heavy on the brake. Thankfully, I don't get stopped by cops. The last thing I need is a ticket. On the way, I get a call from my coworker. She tells me she's sick and it's up to me to handle the presentation on my own. I turn off my phone to try to gather my wits before I walk into the office. My stomach is starting to hurt. I pop an antacid and grab my stuff. As I hurry inside, the chaos of the office crashes through me—detonating telephones, bits of conversation, a barrage of competing cell phones, and the occasional slammed door. The throbbing assault lasts all day.

At lunch, I dash to the drugstore for a prescription. I wait in line. Ten people, nine, eight, eight, eight...

*Come on!*

...Seven, six, five, five, five, five...

*What the?*

Four, three, two, two, *ONE!*

Great. I have ten minutes to get back, which means vending machine garbage for lunch today. I pop another antacid.

After work, I'm running again. Finally at home, I throw dinner together. We scarf it down in silence. Then the children are delivered to activities, retrieved for homework, then bed.

Only to do it all again tomorrow.

# Life's Demands

We all experience varieties of this scenario on a daily basis. Sometimes worse, sometimes better. For many of us, our alarm clock is like a starter pistol that sets us off sprinting through our day. Our many responsibilities and expectations pull us in a hundred different directions that leave us feeling fragmented and ineffective. We are faced with competing demands and challenges. Some may be personal and professional expectations we place on ourselves or others place on us. They may include working long hours, working within dysfunctional systems, and interacting with dysfunctional people. In some instances, the demands placed on us in the workplace increase as our employers expect more and more until we feel there is nothing more to give. Frequently, these expectations are unrealistic.

Personally, we are plagued with interpersonal stressors involving our partners, families, and friends. If we are going to see our partner or a friend, it often requires consciously scheduling time together. Sometimes it is difficult to find time when we are both available. Troubles with family members suffering with illness, personal problems, substance abuse, or other difficulties may tax our time, our money, our patience, and our empathy. Money concerns, such as struggling to pay all the bills and frustration with not being paid enough, also contribute to feelings of inadequacy.

Environmentally, we are ambushed by multitudes of stimuli: traffic, advertising, crowds, sirens, phone calls, texts, public address systems, and thumping music. All this sensory overload may be overwhelming and make us anxious.

Physically, we may have health issues that interfere with our ability to complete the tasks we want to accomplish. We get fatigued and try to fight for each ounce of energy. We may want to be alone and avoid people because we just do not have the energy to interact with anyone. Yet, we may feel lonely. Our breathing is rapid, or we hold our breath. Our shoulders and necks ache after sitting at our computers, working hour after hour. We do not sleep well because we wake in the middle of the night thinking about the future and things to do tomorrow. A sudden realization of, *Uh oh, I forgot to...,* compels us to ruminate on a neglected task rather than get the rest we so desperately require. Our doctors tell us to slow down because our blood pressures are up. Our diets suck. We tend to eat garbage because it is easier and quicker.

Emotionally, we are spent. There is little in reserve to cope with the unexpected. If one more thing gets added to our plates, we feel like we are going to pop. We may find ourselves irritable, angry, or sad. We may cry at the drop of a hat. We may feel more alone than ever, despite the fallacy of immediate connections with technologically linked "friends." We may confront big questions like:

- What is life all about?
- What is the meaning of all this?
- How did I end up living like this?
- Life is too short. Do I really want to live like this?

This experience may be described with one word: **stress.** Over time, we are negatively affected by living in this manner, in which life is living us. Physically, stress may contribute to heart problems, difficulty sleeping, headaches, digestive issues, higher blood pressure, muscle pain, and a whole host of other ailments. Stress may affect how much and what types of food we eat. Stress also contributes to feelings of depression and anxiety. Because of the many detrimental effects of stress, it is vital to consider ways of reducing it in order to live healthier, more satisfying lives.

## Understanding Life's Stress

Given the demands of our busy lives, how do we understand our attempts to cope with life's challenges? How are some of us able to successfully cope while others do not?

There are many ways we may cope with stress, some good and some not so good. Some approach life in a controlled, organized fashion, while others attack life in a haphazard manner. Others cope by relying on alcohol or drugs to "numb" feelings of being overwhelmed. In other instances, people engage in excessive and unhealthy behaviors with sex, exercise, shopping, or eating in an attempt to feel satisfied when they perceive a lack of fulfillment. Technologies like television, video games, social media, and texting are used as a means to escape or avoid stressors.

How well we cope with stress in our lives depends on a psychological concept in social learning theory of personality known as locus of control. Locus of control denotes the extent to which individuals perceive they have the ability to control or impact life choices and decisions. It consists of a continuum between two extremes: internal and external.

Individuals with an internal locus of control rely on themselves and their internal processes, rather than outside influences. They think of themselves as the cause of outcomes in their lives. On the other hand, individuals with an external locus of control look outside themselves for someone or something to protect or guide them in making choices; they rely less on internal processes. These individuals think of external things as the cause of outcomes in their lives.

Individuals who function from an extreme internal locus of control may be described as self-sufficient and very independent. They are unlikely to ask others for help, even if they would benefit from assistance. They are not open to suggestions from others because they are confident they have all the answers for their lives. They are self-reliant and do not depend on others to meet their needs. They strive to direct and manage outcomes.

Individuals who function from an extreme external locus of control may be described as reliant and dependent. They continually ask for help, even though they are quite capable of accomplishing tasks by themselves. They rely on others to tell them what to do and believe they are incapable of making decisions for their lives. They rely on others to meet their needs and believe fate, chance, and luck determine their lives.

Functioning from either extreme is not effective for coping with life's stress. With an extreme internal locus of control, individuals may feel responsible for every aspect of their lives, which may contribute to feelings of inadequacy even though it is not possible to take on everything. With an extreme external locus of control, individuals may feel they are not able to direct their lives and affect their world. This mindset may contribute to feelings of helplessness. Individuals with an extreme internal locus of control at least have a strong sense of identity and may still be effective in making decisions, whereas individuals with an extreme external locus of control may be so dependent they have little sense of identity and are unable to make decisions in their lives.

It is not healthy to be at either extreme. It is equally unhealthy to take too much or too little responsibility for our lives and our choices. We are challenged to develop an internal locus of control that does not rely on others to tell us what to do; we must look within ourselves to make choices and decisions in our own lives.

The goal is to achieve a healthy balance between internal and external locus of control. We want an internal locus of control strong enough that we direct our lives, but not so strong it makes us believe we have control over everything and every situation we encounter. We want an external locus of control strong enough that we appreciate the external pressures, expectations, and responsibilities of daily life, but not so strong we believe everything in every situation has control over us.

# A Model for Living Life Well

In over 20 years of working as a psychologist, I have observed that our hectic schedules often do not allow us time to look within ourselves and address our lives. Our demanding and busy lives take us away from self-reflection and knowing ourselves. The busier we are, the more difficult it is to find the time and energy to focus within ourselves and fully live our lives. But the more demanding our lives, the more important self-reflection becomes. If we are not careful, life lives us, rather than us living life.

The results of my doctoral research served as a springboard for me to understand how individuals may effectively face life's challenges with a balanced locus of control. My years of clinical experience have further impressed upon me its importance. I have found that individuals who successfully maintain a balanced locus of control are more successful in overcoming challenges. Additionally, in facing my own vision loss, it has become clear to me how crucial it is to maintain a balanced locus of control when I process and consider ways I may most effectively and efficiently face everyday challenges. This is especially evident when even the simplest tasks are burdensome and difficult. By maintaining a balanced locus of control, I am able to move through whatever is thrown at me, no matter how frustrating it is.

Over time, I developed the Four Principles for building life satisfaction to effectively achieve a balanced locus of control regardless of stressors or challenges. My dissertation research, clinical experience, and personal experience have all contributed to the development of the Four Principles. With a balanced locus of control, we will greatly increase our ability to successfully overcome and accept any challenge we face in our lives. This balance will enable us to build life satisfaction.

"Life satisfaction" is a nebulous and subjective term that involves many dimensions. It is frequently associated with personality, age, life events and experiences, values, religion, culture, family, career, and so on. The amount of life satisfaction individuals experience may be evidenced by their moods, achieved goals, relationships with others, self-concept, ability to cope with daily life, and favorable attitude. In general, individuals are likely to perceive life satisfaction from their own life perspective.

Individuals who are satisfied with life are likely to demonstrate more flexibility when coping with stressors. They are likely to be more optimistic about the future and experience fewer personal problems. Individuals who are less satisfied with life are likely to be less flexible, feel less optimistic about the future, and experience more personal problems. Others in the field of psychology and psychiatry have also defined life satisfaction as an expression of individuals' coping abilities and subjective states that result from successful and unsuccessful coping skills.

Because life satisfaction is so complex, it is important to regularly evaluate how well we are obtaining what we perceive as a satisfying life. This evaluation helps us to consider and clarify where we are in life and whether we want to make changes and do things differently. Regardless of our current level of life satisfaction, we may all benefit from developing skills and strategies that help us build life satisfaction in our ever-changing environments and circumstances.

This is the daily challenge: How do we address and resolve the multitude of stressors we face in our busy and demanding lives? There are many self-help and personal growth books that present coping strategies, but only some provide a theoretical foundation to explain how and why their strategies are beneficial. *Four Principles for Facing Life's Challenges: A Guide for Making Choices that Build Life Satisfaction* presents a balanced locus of control as a primary component for effectively facing life's challenges and building life satisfaction. The Four Principles provide pathways for achieving this balanced locus of control. They also provide tools for facing stressors and guide you in making choices that build life satisfaction.

Principle I: Self-nurturing and taking care of myself

Principle II: Living in the present

Principle III: Developing a positive relationship with myself

Principle IV: Understanding and recognizing choices in life

I will provide you with skills and strategies to attain each of the Four Principles. I will also present the psychological background in which they are rooted to give you a more comprehensive understanding of how and why they work. I believe if individuals understand the reason why something helps them, they are much more inclined to implement change that leads to improvement in their lives. At the end of each chapter, I will provide opportunities for self-reflection that will enable you to personalize these skills and strategies to make them work best for you.

Now, let us join together on this journey to learn the Four Principles, which lead to a balanced locus of control and allow us to effectively and efficiently face life's challenges. Facing these challenges will ultimately build life satisfaction.

# PRINCIPLE I

---

## Self-Nurturing and Taking Care of Myself

# CHAPTER 2

---

# Filling My Water Pitcher: A Reservoir for Coping

## The Importance of Making Me a Priority

It is important to take care of and nurture ourselves physically, emotionally, and spiritually. This is especially important during periods of stress.

Imagine yourself as a vessel with a pitcher of water inside. The water represents your reservoir for coping with stress. We give this water to other people during the course of our day as we work, relate with others, nurture others, engage in activities, volunteer, and perform all the other things we do that take our energy. If we give too much to our work, our family, our friends, and our activities, our pitcher becomes depleted. When this occurs, our ability to cope with stressors diminishes. We may feel off-balance, irritated, frustrated, overwhelmed, angry, and fatigued, or we may lack energy and motivation. The goal is to find ways to fill our water pitchers so we are better able to cope with our daily stressors.

We are often taught to take care of everyone and everything else before taking care of ourselves. Work, children, partners, friends, household chores, pets, and a litany of other tasks and responsibilities frequently take priority over taking care of ourselves. Even if we place Me on our list of priorities, we are likely to put it at the bottom of that list. It is vital for us to learn to take care of ourselves, first and foremost, so we can be available to the people we love and the things we love to do. Many of us had parents who gave so much of themselves to their families that perhaps they did not model healthy self-care. Through them and others, we may have erroneously learned that if we take care of ourselves first, we are selfish.

In urging you to fill your water pitcher, I am not encouraging selfishness. Selfishness occurs when people fill their water pitcher until it is overflowing. There is no outward flow from their pitchers, and that is selfish narcissism. For these individuals, everything is about them. When encountering selfish people, you may feel as though they have taken a straw and sucked your water pitcher dry, leaving you exhausted and wrung out, with little water to use for coping. If you know individuals who are selfish like this, be aware of the amount of energy they take from you. You may want to make choices that limit your exposure to them to protect the water in your pitcher.

It is important to learn ways to fill your water pitcher so you have resources for coping with stressors. The greater the water in your pitcher, the better you are able to cope with challenges.

However, the goal is not to have a full-to-the-brim pitcher. The goal is to learn to fill yourself up, not only so you have adequate water to cope with stressors, but also to nurture others and engage in activities. The object is to find a healthy exchange of inflow for self-nurturing and outflow for nurturing others and coping with stressful challenges.

# Levels of Self-Nurturing

I have identified three levels of self-nurturing that fill our water pitchers. These levels are primal, play-recreational activities, and naturally occurring phenomena.

## THE PRIMAL LEVEL OF SELF-NURTURING

The primal level of self-nurturing consists of diet, exercise, and sleep.

Diet. I am not a nutritionist or dietitian. It is important to follow any dietary and nutritional recommendations given to you by your physician or medical professional. You are encouraged to seek consultation with dietitians, nutritionists, and other professionals in this area to gain specific knowledge related to the effects of food and nutrition on the body and brain and determine whether you may benefit from special dietary requirements. Be aware that the food we eat fuels our brains.

It is important to recognize how food impacts the sharpness of our minds, the healthiness of our bodies, and—perhaps less obviously but equally important—the stability of our moods.

Caffeine impacts mental health. It spikes energy levels, only for them to crash. Overuse of caffeine may be unintentional. You may get up in the morning and have a cup of coffee to get started. Perhaps you simply enjoy savoring a cup of coffee. It is the taste and the warmth that helps you get ready for your day. However, it is likely you are attracted to coffee because the caffeine drives you to buy or brew a cup. After a few hours you may feel sluggish, so you may grab another cup. If you work a typical day shift, then in the early afternoon you may start to experience a dip in your energy level due to natural circadian rhythms. Dips in energy may drive you to drink caffeine throughout your day, interrupting your ability to sleep when you go to bed.

If you have coffee later in your day, the stimulant effect may interfere with your sleep cycle. It is important to be conscious of the time of day you consume caffeine, so you are not disrupting your natural sleep cycle. I encourage you to discuss with your medical professional what an acceptable amount of caffeine is for you. Individuals who experience anxiety are especially encouraged not to drink caffeine, as the stimulant effect will likely add to feelings of anxiety. Similarly, if your moods are up and down, you may wish to avoid consuming caffeine because it may compound their intensity. If you are struggling with stress or if you are feeling down, you may also be attracted to caffeine to boost your energy. Try not to be drawn to the effects of the initial energy boost, as it will not last. Instead, eating foods high in protein may raise your energy level, maintaining it without spiking it. A nutritionist, dietitian, or medical professional may help you determine the healthiest snacks for you.

Our need for an energy boost may encourage us to snack on something sweet without really thinking about what we are stuffing in our mouths. We hope this snack will sustain us, but instead we soon experience a drop in our energy level. We are just as tired as we were before, or even more so. Remember, chocolate has caffeine in it.

Exercise. Exercise is obviously important for physical health, as it gets our hearts pumping, our respiratory systems working, our muscles strengthening, and so on. Regular exercise improves stamina, controls weight, builds strength, and improves longevity.

Exercise is also an important component of maintaining good mental health and managing stress. All emotion has energy associated with it. If we do not have an opportunity to express our emotion, it may become internalized. The energy may become stale and stagnant, contributing to feeling tied up inside, frustrated, and edgy. Often after moderate to strenuous exercise we think, *Oh, wow! I feel so good now. I feel like a different person!* Feeling rejuvenated and like "a new person" typifies the effect of releasing old, stale emotional energy. Before you exercised, you might have questioned whether you were going to take the time to work out. Times when we **least** want to exercise are actually the **most** important times to do so, because it releases our pent-up emotional energy and revitalizes us.

Regular exercise releases endorphins. Some individuals talk about experiencing a "runner's high" to denote the effects of endorphins being released. Endorphins are our body's natural healing agents. They assist in combating physical illness and injury, and likely also serve to combat depression, anxiety, and stress. The euphoria from released endorphins may make us lose track of time. The adage "time flies when we're having fun" often comes from a flow of endorphins.

There are strong indications that exercise may stabilize mood. Many people tell me that when they are regularly exercising, they perceive their moods are less erratic and they feel calmer. They believe exercise is important in leveling their moods. They perceive getting regular exercise leads to feeling greater balance and improves their ability to cope with daily stressors and unexpected challenges.

It is important, when choosing an exercise program, to consult with your medical professionals and follow their guidelines to ensure safe participation in your chosen activity. Find a way to exercise that is fun for you. If your workout is an onerous chore, then it is less likely you will regularly exercise. Engaging in a variety of different activities reduces the possibility of experiencing monotony and boredom. Some possibilities for variety are joining a local sports league, working with a personal trainer, creating a workout schedule with a friend, walking your dog, hiking a mountain, joining a fun run, or learning a new sport. The bottom line is getting up, getting active, and having fun.

I strongly caution against a "New Year's resolution exercise program" involving a sudden high-intensity exercise regime, especially if exercise has not been a consistent part of your life. Sudden increases in activity may result in you feeling so sore and uncomfortable you do not want to continue exercising. Start small, even if it is only a walk down the block and back. Any exercise is better than none. The key is to regularly exercise so it becomes a habit and gives you a chance to recognize the beneficial effects on your mental health.

Sleep. Sleep is one of the most natural ways we nurture ourselves. If we do not get good sleep, we may experience depression, anxiety, and stress. While each of us may require different amounts, it is vital to everyone's mental health to have enough sleep. Our brain requires it in order to decompress from the stress of the day. Without sufficient sleep, our ability to cope with life's challenges will diminish.

To support adequate sleep it is important to address our behaviors associated with sleep, known as "sleep hygiene." Here are some pointers that may help you get the sleep you and your brain require.

Keep a regular sleep-wake cycle. Going to bed and waking at consistent times teaches our body when to be asleep and when to be awake. An irregular sleep schedule causes stress, as our body is being asked to be active when it thinks it is expected to be resting and resting when it thinks it is expected to be active. A consistent sleep schedule helps to ensure adequate rest.

Avoid ruminating on future tasks when you are preparing for bed. A common pitfall for many of us is thinking about all there is to do tomorrow when we are washing our faces and brushing our teeth. Bedtime is not the time to think about tomorrow. It is the time to think about sleeping, unwinding, and slowing down our thoughts. Practice using the evening to slow down and let go of the day. If you have clothes to organize and papers to prepare for tomorrow, take care of them early enough in the evening to allow time—preferably a couple of hours—to relax and unwind. As you prepare for bed, tell yourself, *This is my time to sleep. This is my time to relax.* If you have intrusive thoughts about all there is to do tomorrow, remind yourself, *I'm not thinking about tomorrow. This is my time to rest.*

If you wake up in the middle of the night worried about all that is not done and all there is to do, do not lie there stewing about it. Keep a pen and paper on your nightstand. If you wake up worried about something, write down your concerns so you will not stress about forgetting them. It is easy to mull over and over in your mind, *I hope I don't forget to get those things done,* and become so preoccupied you are unable to get back to sleep. Writing down these thoughts frees your mind. You will have a list the next morning to remind you of things to be done, rather than burdening your brain to remember everything when you are trying to sleep. Ironically, it is often the case that when we look at the list in the morning, we wonder, *Why was this important enough for me to wake up and worry last night?* What kept us awake in the dark of night may appear trivial in the light of day.

Another common difficulty is being tempted to get up and do something when we wake up in the middle of the night, rather than lying awake in bed. Doing a load of laundry, dusting, or grabbing a midnight snack may sound productive, but instead these activities significantly hinder our ability to establish a healthy sleep routine. If we get up at night multiple times in a row, we risk the possibility of creating a habit so our brain and our body thinks, *It's two o'clock in the morning. It's time to get up and do some chores.* The better thing to do is stay in bed and slow down your thoughts. Focus on pleasant things, listen to soothing music, meditate, or do a relaxation exercise. The goal is to turn off your brain and get back to sleep. Getting up, doing chores, or eating only serve to wake up our brains.

Another important consideration for sleep is being aware of our activities and what we do before bedtime. I choose not to watch the evening news because I do not want to take negativity to bed with me. To stay informed, I listen to the morning news so I have all day to process any negativity I encounter in today's news broadcast. It is important to recognize that we have control over what we expose ourselves to. If we are not careful, we may easily become overwhelmed by the world's barrage of intrusive negativity. Newscasts, music lyrics, movies, television, video games, social media, and books can inundate us with boundless tragedies, disasters, corruption, and crimes. Listen to yourself. If you find that something is stressing you, choose to manage your exposure to it. Carefully consider your pre-bedtime entertainment, because you take with you to sleep what you were doing just prior to switching off the light. Your brain continues to process what it was last exposed to just before going to sleep.

For many people, reading before bedtime is a wonderful way to unwind from the day and transition to sleep. Again, it is important to consider and choose what material you read prior to sleep. Reading action thrillers, murder mysteries, or other exciting or upsetting material is not conducive for sleep. These materials may stimulate our thoughts and emotions. Consider reading something that is uplifting, positive, or educational that will mellow your mood and allow you to drift off into a peaceful, restful sleep.

Food also plays a role in achieving quality sleep. Allowing your body adequate time to digest a meal is important. That may be difficult if your bedtime closely follows the end of your work schedule. It is not uncommon for me to work late into the evening. I have learned that I sleep better if I eat a lighter meal in the evening and, if at all possible, have my main meal during the day. You may want to avoid certain foods just before bedtime. Spicy meals or sweets may disrupt your digestion, and the resulting discomfort or energy boost may keep you awake.

Sleeping in a cool room is typically more conducive than sleeping in a warm room. Usually, it is better to sleep in a darker environment. It is also better to sleep in an environment without nightlights or light that creeps in from streetlights. Digital clocks may produce enough glare to interfere with sleep. Noise often contributes to sleep loss as well. Street noise, activities of family members, and pets may jolt you awake or keep you from deep sleep. If light and noise interfere with your sleep, using an eye mask and earplugs may block the intrusion of unwanted stimuli. Sometimes just running a fan to produce consistent ambient noise will mask the noise outside your bedroom.

Something less obvious may also be impeding quality sleep. There is some evidence suggesting blue light emitted from devices with screens may interfere with sleep patterns. Avoiding electronics prior to bedtime may help you drift off more quickly.

Ask yourself what works best for you. The key here is to recognize that your behaviors and choices may influence how well you sleep. If you find yourself dragging during the day, your body may be telling you that you are not getting enough quality sleep. If you are getting adequate hours of sleep and are still feeling fatigued, I encourage you to consult with a medical professional to explore other possible reasons for your lack of energy.

## THE PLAY-RECREATIONAL ACTIVITIES LEVEL OF SELF-NURTURING

The play-recreational activities level of self-nurturing involves anything you do for fun. It may be a brief activity like reading a daily meditation, or doing something all day or for several days, such as boating, camping, hiking, or taking a road trip. It is not necessary for play-recreational activities to be active in the sense of strenuous exertion. They may be sedentary activities like reading, drawing, painting, or listening to music. They are active in the sense that we are actively choosing to engage in something simply because it is fun and gives us pleasure.

Other self-nurturing activities may include enjoying a bubble bath, taking time for primping, getting a pedicure or manicure, treating ourselves to a massage, gardening, cooking, putting puzzles together, working on vehicles, making music, coloring in coloring books, joining a fantasy football league, refinishing furniture, woodworking, making crafts, participating in sports—the list goes on and on. There are so many ways to have fun that are self-nurturing. These activities may also include what we typically call hobbies. The key here is the word "play." For many of us, as we grow up, we forget how to have fun for fun's sake. We become so responsible we often neglect to take time to allow ourselves to play.

There are two things to consider when we engage in play-recreational activities. The first thing to consider is that play is for fun. The best models for play are children. They are spontaneous, creative, and carefree. Responsibilities, regimented thought, and self-consciousness do not hinder their ability to find and have fun. As we become adults, we may believe we no longer have time for fun. We are consumed with meeting expectations like graduating from school, having a successful career, providing for a family, paying bills, and fulfilling a multitude of other responsibilities. There is so much to do and there never seems to be enough time to do it all.

Time and pressures may keep us from having fun, as do fear of the unknown and fear of looking silly. Maybe you were terrible at art in school. Your drawings looked like drunken stick figures. Your sculptures resembled molten slag. Maybe you sang like a screech owl in chorus. You danced with the grace of a hobbled mule at a sock hop. All these perceived past failures and embarrassments may keep you from daring to try new things or from artistically expressing yourself. Unkind judgments and ridicule may have left you believing that having fun has little value or is just not right for you. However, play—having fun for fun's sake—provides a crucial avenue for self-nurturing.

Here is a personal example. Once I completed my doctorate, I realized I was not taking time to play. I always wanted to learn how to throw pottery. At the time, I had two choices: I could take a course at the community college, or I could attend a class at the local recreation center. I immediately decided against taking a class at the community college. The idea of taking a course threatened to throw me back into academic performance mode, and my whole goal was to break out of that. The moment grades, projects, or deadlines were associated with my performance, I knew I would strive to excel instead of appreciating the experience and having fun. So, I went to the local recreation center and took their pottery class. But me being me, I knew I would struggle to abandon my penchant for being a goal-driven, organized, responsible adult.

To avoid the killjoy aspects of being exclusively focused on production during the class, I used my organizational talents to make a contract with myself to ensure I enjoyed the time and learned how to have fun again. My contract stipulated that I relished the clay, felt the clay oozing through my fingers, noticed the coolness of the clay on my skin, and enjoyed the clay's softness. I was mandated to squish to oblivion no fewer than three of my creations to reinforce that this was about fun and not about production or achievement. Also, my contract bound me to color my masterpieces in vibrant, pleasing shades that I was able to see even though they might clash with the décor of my home. Never mind that some people may have giggled and smirked at the objects I created, which looked like they had been made by a colorblind wombat wearing mittens! The point was that I had fun and allowed myself to be present with the experience. I keep these trophies to remind myself of my victory—of learning that I am a goal-driven, organized, responsible adult, who is also able to have fun.

The second thing to consider when we engage in play is the attitude with which we approach an activity. Our attitude significantly impacts an activity's ability to be nurturing. Our attitude involves locus of control. To review, there is an internal and an external locus of control. If I watch my favorite 30-minute sitcom and then turn it off when it is over, then who is in control? I am. This is an example of an internal locus of control. If I have 20 minutes to play a video game and find myself playing it for 5 hours, trying to get to the next level, who is in control? Me or the video game? The video game. This is an example of external locus of control.

Why is this distinction so important? Because we know that an **internal** locus of control is healthier. It promotes the perspective that **I** am making choices for my life. **I** am making decisions. **I** am in the driver's seat. An **internal** locus of control supports health and well-being, while an **external** locus of control promotes depression, anxiety, and stress. Therefore, while engaging in play-recreational activities, it is important to consider whether I am controlling the activity or the activity is controlling me.

Let us say I am knitting a scarf and I only have two inches left to finish. It is one o'clock in the morning. If I tell myself, *By golly Cheryl, whether you're tired or not you will finish this,* then I have an external locus of control. Something outside of me is trying to control me. If I tell myself, *I'm tired. I'm going to go to bed, and I'll get back to that scarf whenever I'm able*, I have an internal locus of control. It is important to strive for an internal locus of control so **you** make choices, not only in your play-recreational activities, but in **all** aspects of your life.

When an activity becomes external in locus, it becomes work, not play. A golfer who throws his club in anger over a missed putt is focused on his performance and his score. It is beyond me to understand how golfing is nurturing when this type of behavior occurs. Performance is usually an external locus. Enjoying the day and doing our best at playing golf is an internal locus. People who are learning how to play the piano may be engaging in a play-recreational activity when they are enjoying the process of learning something new. As they advance in proficiency, they may strive to improve their ability. If they place expectations on their performance, playing the piano may become work and lose its ability to nurture.

I am not suggesting it is not okay to strive to perform well. It becomes a problem, however, when we put expectations on our performance. Expectations result in an external locus of control. Recognizing when our fun, our hobbies, and our passions shift from being sources of enjoyment to sources of disappointment and stress determines whether an activity is self-nurturing. Pounding the keys and shrieking is a sure sign your burgeoning piano skills are more about achievement and expectations than self-nurturing. If the neighbors are complaining about loud bangs and swearing, it is probably time to reassess how nurturing your play-recreational activities truly are.

## THE NATURALLY OCCURRING PHENOMENA LEVEL OF SELF-NURTURING

This level of self-nurturing includes activities and experiences that involve our senses—sight, hearing, smell, taste, and touch. We use our senses to appreciate naturally occurring phenomena. Opportunities for this appreciation constantly surround us. By heightening our awareness of the beauty in our environment, we find ways to nurture ourselves.

Pausing to watch the sparkle as snow drifts down. Taking a stroll to view the colors of changing leaves in the fall. Spotting deer grazing in a field. Halting to listen to the burble of water flowing through a creek. Stopping to smell freshly cut grass. Savoring the flavors of a specially cooked meal. Reveling in a warm ray of sunshine on a brisk day. Taking a moment to stroke a beloved pet. All these and more are nurturing natural phenomena.

Contrary to the name, naturally occurring phenomena do not exclusively involve nature. There are myriad ways to appreciate your environment in urban areas. Appreciating an interesting building or sculpture, enjoying the aroma of cooking food, listening to catchy street music, or delighting in a lively market might all provide moments of self-nurturing. The "nature" in naturally occurring phenomena simply means the environment you are in at this moment. It is not necessary to leave where you are to discover or appreciate something nurturing. Just stop and heighten your awareness to consciously appreciate things you may find beautiful, meaningful, and interesting.

Appreciating naturally occurring phenomena may lead you to feel more alive and connected to the world. It may lead you to feel excited and enthralled with the beauty all around you. Stopping to notice little things that are nurturing is an excellent way to slow down your thoughts, steer you away from the demands of the day, and get off the treadmill of life—if only for a few moments. Naturally occurring phenomena let you catch your breath before you get back on that treadmill.

Appreciating naturally occurring phenomena takes only moments and costs nothing. The old adage "stop to smell the roses" is actually an important guide to our well-being. In our very busy lives, we may get so absorbed with trudging along on the never-ending treadmill of life that we are hesitant to stop, get off, and look around. Sometimes the treadmill may seem more like a hamster wheel—the harder we try to keep up, the faster the wheel spins. Our treadmill will go as fast as we allow it. This makes stopping that much more important, because it affords us the opportunity to take a breath, which in turn keeps us from feeling our life is out of control.

When focusing on goals, responsibilities, and chores, it is easy to perceive the world in tunnel vision, which only allows us to see what we think we need to get done. When we obsess with getting from Point A to Point B, we are blinded to all the things around us that may be nurturing. I encourage you to make the choice to regularly step off the treadmill of life and appreciate what is nurturing all around you.

Let me describe aspects of my treadmill of life and how I use naturally occurring phenomena for self-nurturing. The days I see clients are often booked solid from 8:00 a.m. to 7:00 p.m. Between client sessions, there are phone calls to return, appointments to schedule, paperwork to complete, and a whole host of other demands on my time and attention. With all this going on—and my brain packed with things to be done now, things to be done before the end of the day, and things to be done in the near future—I consciously stop throughout my day to appreciate the naturally occurring phenomena I have deliberately placed around me. In my office, I have chosen colors that are soothing for me and my clients. Pictures of my past guide dogs fill me with fond memories of their antics and never fail to evoke a smile. My favorite naturally occurring phenomenon is a moment with my guide dog. A smooch and a few rubs of his fur help me disconnect and have a warm, fuzzy moment. Please note that my appreciation for naturally occurring phenomena literally takes only seconds. The same will be true for you.

I have developed an attitude that no matter where I am, or no matter what I am doing, I will take a few seconds to recognize naturally occurring phenomena that are nurturing to me. When I am at the grocery store, I like to go through the flower section to see the beautiful colors and enjoy the pleasing fragrances. When I take my guide dog out to do his business, I use his deliberateness in finding just the right spot as an opportunity to appreciate the warm sun on my face, the sound of birds singing, and the fragrance of lilacs filling my nose.

Things that delay and irritate us may be used as unexpected opportunities to appreciate the world around us. Waiting in a supermarket checkout line is aggravating, especially if we are in a hurry. However, any time we are forced to stop is an opportunity to self-nurture. We may consciously redirect our frustrations at a slow-moving line into finding something nurturing in our environment. Rather than tapping our foot or shouting, *Hurry up!,* in our minds, we may enjoy looking at colorful balloons or toys, smelling freshly baked bread or a floral display, and chuckling at the tabloid headlines at the newsstand.

## Self-Reflection

By consciously taking moments to self-nurture on all levels—primal, play-recreational activities, and naturally occurring phenomena—you will fill your coping water pitcher so you may more effectively face the day's challenges.

Take time to nurture yourself repeatedly throughout your day. Opportunities may take only seconds, such as when you appreciate an interesting cloud, pet a pet, listen to a bird's song, or feel the warmth of a sunny day. Also, make a conscious effort to engage in lengthier self-nurturing activities, such as exercising, playing, or just doing something for you. No matter where you are, and no matter what you are doing, it is important to be open to beautiful things and nurturing activities that fill up your water pitcher.

Consider ways you nurture yourself on all levels: primal, play-recreational, and naturally occurring phenomena. I recommend writing down how you nurture yourself so you may concretely identify nurturing activities. This list will lead to greater awareness of your nurturing activities and when you are nurturing yourself. I suggest you also list activities you have wanted to try but have put off. Try the activities on this list to determine if you find them nurturing. You may add to the number of ways you nurture yourself. Be open to trying new things. There may be a whole host of new activities you find fun, enjoyable, and nurturing.

Telling yourself, *I don't have time,* is not an option. You may be struggling with facing life's challenges because you are not making time to nurture yourself and fill your water pitcher. Let me provide an example from my life to illustrate the importance of **making** time to nurture myself. I vividly remember a time in graduate school when I was studying for an eight-chapter test. After poring over the first four chapters, I wanted a break. Part of me said, *I want to go for a swim. A swim will relax and refresh me so I may breeze through the last four chapters.* Another part of me said, *I don't have time to waste swimming. I need to get this done.*

What were my options? I might forge ahead with my studying when I was tired, but it would be more difficult to learn the information. Or I might make time for myself by taking a break to go for a swim, which would refill my water pitcher and reenergize me to attack the next four chapters. I decided to swim and felt so refreshed that I easily completed studying the remaining chapters. Had I not gone swimming, I would have been pushing myself too hard. I would not have been as effective and efficient in my learning. I use this experience to remind myself that we are much better off when we make time to nurture ourselves and refill our water pitcher, rather than pressing on when we are empty and depleted.

It is important to regularly invest in self-nurturing. Making small amounts of time for it throughout your day will provide you with continual payoff in energy to face challenges you encounter. If you do not take time to consistently fill your pitcher with self-nurturing, you may become depleted and too tired to effectively face your challenges. If you find yourself pushing forward with a task when you are tired and exhausted, it may be constructive to give yourself permission to take a small amount of time to engage in a nurturing activity. After you take a break, go back to the task. You will likely be more productive.

When we are sick or feeling unwell, our water pitchers are more quickly depleted. Our coping resources go into our bodies for healing. This explains why many of us may become grumpy or irritable when we do not feel well. We have a smaller reservoir for coping. Those of you who struggle with pain know only too well how quickly your water pitcher is depleted when you have a bad day. The same is true for me. Using my residual vision for any length of time depletes my water pitcher more quickly than anything else. Identify what drains you the most. If you know what especially drains you, you will be more effective in finding ways to compensate. If I have a day when there are heavy demands on my residual vision, I not only deliberately set aside extra time to have no visual stimulation, I also engage in self-nurturing activities that do not require vision, such as going for a swim, listening to music, reading a braille book, or giving my guide dog extra belly rubs. These activities allow me to fill my water pitcher and face whatever challenges the rest of my day brings. If I do not take this extra time, then not only may I experience headaches, I will also feel fatigued, wrung out, and spent.

Self-nurturing also keeps us in the present. If I am enjoying how soft the upholstery is on my armchair, there is no place for me to be but in this moment, this second. If I am petting my guide dog, I am appreciating how soft his fur is and how bad his breath smells. I am not thinking about the phone calls I will make or the piles of paperwork lurking on my desk. While self-nurturing, we are in the moment of appreciating the experience. We are not dwelling on what has happened or worrying about what will happen. We are experiencing just this moment. Self-nurturing offers us the opportunity to learn to be in the present.

This realization takes us right to the second of the Four Principles: Living in the present.

# PRINCIPLE II

## Living in the Present

# CHAPTER 3

---

# Maneuvering Through Time, Setting Goals, and Learning from Experience

Consider these two statements:

1. If I am living in the future or the past,
   I am not living my life.

2. If I am not living in the present,
   I am not fully living my life.

Where do you live in time? The healthiest place for us to live is the present. If we live in the future or the past, we are unable to fully experience our lives. Living in the future or the past each has its own set of difficulties.

# Future Orientation

What happens if you propel yourself into the future? Take a moment to reflect on what sorts of feelings come up for you when you think about it. You might ask yourself, *What if this...? What if that...?* You may feel fear, dread, apprehension, anticipation, excitement, worry, nervousness, and anxiousness. You may feel overwhelmed. All these are emotional descriptors of anxiety. If you live in the future, you are likely to experience anxiety. Even if you are excited about something good, it is a type of anxiety. The common perception is that anxiety always comes from negative events. However, anxiety may come from positive life events like graduating from school, getting married, landing a new job, having a baby, buying a new house, and so on.

Do you know what is going to happen in the future? Most of you will say no. If you say yes, please send me some stock picks or lottery numbers! Many of the choices we make today are in preparation for positive events in the future, such as saving for our kids' college, buying a new home, traveling, and planning for retirement. Some choices are intended to lessen the negative effects of some future event, such as buying insurance for our cars, our homes, or our health. The most effective way to actively achieve what we want is to make choices today that are consistent with what we want for our tomorrow. In other words, I want to invest today in what I want for my tomorrow.

When I ask an adolescent male what his goals are, he may say, "I want to be a doctor or a lawyer." If his behavior and choices are not consistent with this goal, I may point out to him that drinking, drugging, procrastinating, and skipping classes are not going to get him where he says he wants to be. "Gee, I never thought about that!" is frequently his response. This is where goals come in. While living in the future is not recommended and creates anxiety, it is important to establish goals to focus our behavior and choices each day. Goals—even minor, easily achievable ones—motivate our behavior toward accomplishing what we want for our lives.

It does not matter how big or small the goals are that we make for ourselves. They may involve major life-changing events, moderate life-improving habits, or minor daily tasks. If I want to achieve a major goal, such as earning a bachelor's degree, I will focus on getting good grades in high school. I will complete the admission requirements for my chosen school. I will secure the funding for my tuition and fees. I will focus on completing each semester of course work. Within each step is a myriad of smaller goals that ensure achieving the primary goal of graduating from college.

If I have a moderate goal, like always getting to work on time, I will limit my TV viewing to ensure I get enough sleep. I will pick out my clothes for the next day before I go to bed. I will place all the things I want to take with me by the door. I may also set my alarm a few minutes earlier to give me a little extra time.

If I have a minor goal, like getting up for the day when the alarm goes off, I will place the alarm far enough away that it forces me to get out of bed to shut it off. I will push myself to get in the shower and get dressed to resist the temptation of slipping back between the sheets.

Goals provide us with the opportunity to feel effective in our lives. Even the smallest accomplishment provides momentum and builds on success. Avoid minimizing the importance of accomplishing minor steps, because they provide the building blocks of our goals. Successfully meeting goals gives us feelings of accomplishment and effectiveness, which promote self-confidence. Self-confidence, in turn, creates momentum for achieving additional goals.

For example, many of us set a goal to lose weight. In the process of losing weight, it is important to be present while making choices concerning diet and exercise. With each successful day of healthy choices and resulting weight loss, self-confidence increases and builds momentum for further weight loss. For some individuals, if they make one error in diet or skip a workout, they throw up their hands and give in to the temptation of bad food choices. They stay on the couch and abandon their goal of losing weight. The healthier way to cope with this setback is recognizing that a mistake has been made and picking up where they left off.

If we have tried but remain unsuccessful in meeting our goals, we have an opportunity to recognize the importance of additional changes in our behavior and choices. An unmet goal is not to be judged as a failure. An unmet goal may instead be instrumental in showing us the importance of approaching our goal differently. Many times, a goal requires multiple attempts to gain success. Think of Edison's persistence in the face of his many failures to get his light bulb to glow. The old adage, "If at first you don't succeed, try, try again," accurately describes the importance of not being discouraged by setbacks.

When we set out to achieve our goals, we make choices. For example, when I agree to give a presentation at a conference, I make a series of choices to ensure I am adequately prepared. The same day I agree to present, I begin writing an outline of the topics I will introduce. Once I am satisfied with my outline, I develop my presentation. When that is finished, I consider potential questions participants may ask. I review current literature to accurately answer their questions. If the presentation is at a major conference, I rehearse and time it to ensure it is clear and abides by the program schedule. By doing all this practice and preparation, there is plenty of opportunity to hone my presentation. By constructively using the time before I step up to the podium, I am less anxious because I know I have done all I am able to be ready for my presentation. Thus, I have done today all I am able to do to achieve my goal for tomorrow.

Taking this example a step further, suppose that when I check in at the conference center the organizer tells me, "Cheryl, I know I asked you to do a 90-minute presentation, but I made a mistake and put you in the program for three hours." Once the initial wave of anxiety washes over me and I catch my breath, I recognize it is my choice to accommodate this sudden request or stick to the original agreement. Because of the thoroughness of my preparation, my comfort level with the material gives me the confidence to extend the presentation, if it is something I want to do. I may choose not to do a longer presentation, but this decision is a personal choice, not one dictated by anxiety resulting from feeling unprepared. This example demonstrates that if I am fully prepared today for what I am planning for tomorrow, I will be much more confident and capable of overcoming life's unexpected challenges.

Some of us overzealously plan for the future. Some excessively plan, trying to account for every conceivable way something might go wrong. However, having some sort of contingency plan, some potential solutions for when things do not go according to plan, will reduce anxiety. Take the example of the conference. I want to ensure that when I step up to the podium, I have my slides ready to go. To ensure I am all set, I bring my presentation with me on a flash drive. In case I lose my flash drive or it gets damaged during my trip, I make sure the conference organizer already has a copy of my presentation. In case the organizer does not have my presentation, I have my flash drive ready to go. These are simple Plan A and Plan B scenarios that make me more comfortable and less anxious, because I know I am taking reasonable steps to ensure everything is ready at the appointed time.

Some people have a Plan A through Plan Z. They try to predict every little thing that may go wrong. With a presentation, they may have a litany of frets and worries. *Will the projector work? What if the bulb burns out halfway through the presentation? Will the microphone make my voice loud enough? Will the podium be too short or too high...or will there be a podium at all? Will they think to provide me with water? What if my voice fails? What if I start sneezing or get the hiccups?* The list of what ifs goes on and on. This kind of extreme contingency planning is living in the future and promotes anxiety through excessive worry. If you are feeling overwhelmed and anxious while planning for a future event, ask yourself whether you are living in the present or overwhelming yourself with potential what ifs.

Let us consider something we all worry about: money. Many of us make choices today to plan for our financial future. We may invest in stocks, bonds, real estate, precious metals, or our cousin Vinnie's surefire-can't-miss investment opportunity. We do the best we are able, investing in what we perceive are secure options for our future. We gather information, we seek a variety of opinions, and we make the best decisions possible given the information available today. We make these choices hoping events in the future will be profitable. But as we all know, the future is not always predictable. The stock markets may tumble, bonds may default, new mines may cheapen our precious metals, real estate bubbles may burst, and good old cousin Vinnie may not know a darn thing about running a business. While we may plan for a profitable tomorrow, our future may turn out quite differently than we had hoped.

If unforeseen events make a shambles of your investment strategies, the healthiest course of action is to address these circumstances as they arise. Negative or disastrous events may happen, but the goal of staying in the present is to not waste energy worrying about every little thing that may negatively affect your assets. Staying up all night worrying about predicted weather patterns—which may increase weevil populations, which may reduce crop production, which may diminish the profits of one-tenth of one percent of the holdings in one of your large cap mutual funds—is an absurd waste of energy. This type of living in the future will only increase your anxiety and lead you to feeling overwhelmed, ineffective, and inadequate. It may also negatively affect your physical health by raising your blood pressure, increasing muscle tension, and—in the worst-case scenario—leading to panic attacks.

It is impossible to account for every circumstance. Again, the healthiest way to overcome unexpected challenges is to address them as they arise. Certainly, you may lose money. Unfortunately, the loss may be significant, and we all know that bad things may happen. Address challenges, learn from them, and move forward with your life. The key is that while it is good to develop educated strategies for improving our lives and important to plan for the future, it is crucial to stay present in the present to be healthy. **We are only able to be effective in the present.** We are unable to predict the future. It is only in this moment, at this second, that we are able to take action to affect our lives.

A healthy way to approach the future is through establishing goals. Ask yourself, *What are my goals?* Goals direct your present behavior. They assist you in making choices today that are consistent with what you want tomorrow. If you find yourself living in the future, ask yourself this question: *What may I do today to make my tomorrow what I want it to be?* In other words, invest today in what you want for tomorrow.

# Past Orientation

What happens if you are living in the past? Take a moment to reflect on what sorts of feelings come up when you think about the past. You might lament, "I should have...," "I wish I had...." You may experience heavy feelings of regret, guilt, remorse, disappointment, rejection, betrayal, abandonment, and loneliness. You may experience nostalgic memories of happiness, love, achievement, joy, security, and success. A pitfall of nostalgia is that you may use pleasant memories to highlight the perception that today is not as good as yesterday. Be aware that your treasured, rosy memories of yesteryear may intrude on your ability to be in the present. Ask yourself, *Are my memories inhibiting my ability to experience present happiness?*

There is a significant difference between having treasured pictures of family members on the wall and living in the past, where one fails to appreciate the present. Do you know someone who is always lamenting about all that is wrong with today, how the country is going down the tubes, how we have lost our values and direction? For them, everything was better in the past. Their fondness for what **was** prevents them from appreciating the good in what **is**. Even if we live in fond memories, they may be a source of current discontentment and unhappiness.

For many of us, we dwell on things that did not work out or were unpleasant when we think about the past. Staying in the past, mulling over and ruminating about events that have happened to us, contributes to feelings of depression. The past may serve as an anchor, holding us back from living our lives. It is important to break away from living in the past so we are able to live in the present. Breaking our connection with the past offers us opportunities to make changes in our lives. Finding ways to cut the threads of our past frees us to make healthier and more beneficial choices today. The way to free ourselves from the binding threads of our past is to focus on today being a new day, a new time, and perhaps a new beginning. For individuals who have experienced trauma, breaking away from the past may be more challenging and best addressed with a professional in therapy.

What do we do with our feelings about the past? We know we are unable to change the past. However, we are able to learn from our experiences and use that information when we face similar circumstances today. From the time we are infants to the time we are elderly, our challenge is to learn from our experiences, learn from our mistakes, and use our acquired wisdom to make better choices. People who live effective and efficient lives are those who learn from their life experiences. We all make mistakes. Unfortunately, many of us perceive mistakes as failures. However, making mistakes offers us valuable opportunities to learn important lessons.

A memorable incident with my previous guide dog, Reece, springs to my mind when I think about learning from my own mistakes. One evening, I prepared a special dinner to nurture myself. It was not for any special reason, but I knew it would be a good way to fill up my water pitcher. Delicious baked lemon salmon, fresh steamed vegetables, and pasta with garlic sauce was to be my sumptuous meal. I spent the day fantasizing about how good it would all taste. I lovingly prepared each ingredient, savoring the aromas and licking my lips in anticipation. The meal was finally done, but it was too hot to enjoy. I set my plate on the stove top to cool and took a quick trip upstairs. Moments later, I returned with my stomach growling in expectation. I reached for my dinner. It took a few seconds for my brain to appreciate the surprising lightness of my plate. My meal—my beautiful, long-hoped-for dinner—was gone! And so was my guide dog, Reece.

I called, "Reece? Reece!? Reece!!" I was ticked off and he knew it, but he didn't care. His belly was full of delicious baked lemon salmon, fresh steamed vegetables, and pasta with garlic sauce. But what was I to do? His devouring of my dinner was in the past. There was no way for me to change it. While I slurped a bowl of unsatisfying canned soup, I resolved to learn from this mistake. I would never again leave food within jaws reach of my rapacious hound.

I would like to tell you I absolutely learned this lesson and learned it well. However, Reece was a crafty character and—quite frankly—a bit of a pig (I say this in the most loving way). That Christmas, while I was baking, the little stinker methodically snatched cookies I lay on the counter to cool. Another time, he ate an entire loaf of still-warm banana bread while I was thanking my friend who brought it to me. I eventually learned that anything to do with food required absolute vigilance when my beloved Reece was anywhere in the vicinity.

My experiences with Reece show that learning from mistakes sometimes takes time and may come after several hard lessons. The more quickly we learn from our experiences, the more effective we are in life.

In my opinion, **there is no such thing as failure in life. The only failure in life is not to live it.** I frequently address this topic with parents regarding interactions with their children. I ask parents to allow their children to make mistakes so they may learn from them. Allowing children to make mistakes and fall short of their expectations teaches them to cope with life's challenges. Ashley's not making the varsity team or Jordan's not getting the lead in the school play gives them an opportunity to process disappointment, live through it, and move on. Parents are in a prime position to assist their children in learning problem-solving skills and developing solutions for their problems. When we allow children to face and address challenges at a young age, we provide them with opportunities to develop the skills to effectively cope later in life.

Those parents who swoop down and take away consequences for their children's choices and behavior are not allowing their children to learn ways to problem-solve, develop coping strategies, and learn effective ways of maneuvering through life. I tell parents **now** is the time to allow their children to make mistakes, while they are available to assist their children in developing problem-solving skills. If we take the consequences of mistakes away, the opportunity for learning from them is lost. I believe insulating young people from consequences produces young adults with diminished skills for coping with financial responsibilities, reduced ability to deal with personal or professional setbacks, and inadequate problem-solving skills. Making mistakes is not a bad thing. The key is if, and how, we learn from our mistakes and gain effective skills for facing our present challenges.

## THE TORNADO ANALOGY AND THE PAST

Imagine I find a house I really like and hope to buy. I am able to afford it, the location is perfect, and the neighborhood suits me. I buy the house. Twenty years go by. My family and I make the house into the home we always dreamed of. We share twenty years of Christmas celebrations, Thanksgiving feasts, birthday and graduation parties, family dinners, barbecues, and all sorts of gatherings. It is our safe and cozy shelter from the trials of the outside world.

One day, seemingly like any other day, everyone is at work or at school when a storm brews, spawning tornadoes that blow away our house.

Here is my question: Was I wrong for buying the house?

Most of us would say, "Of course not! You had 20 years of living in the home. You have wonderful memories. You had no way of knowing, when you bought the house, that it would be destroyed by a tornado."

If we impose our present reality onto the past and say, "I should never have bought that house because a tornado blew it away," then we are being irrational and employing a cognitive distortion. Our journey through time is linear. When we bought the house, the tornado did not exist. When we take a present reality and impose it on a past decision, it creates stress. Kicking ourselves for decisions in the past that have subsequently been undone by the unexpected is fruitless. This cognitive distortion leads to feelings of inadequacy.

We are able to act and make choices based only on information available at the time we make a decision. None of us has a crystal ball to predict what will happen in the future. Our journey through life is a path made by choices we make, given the information available at the time. As we go along, new information reveals itself and new events occur, which may lead us to make different choices. The result is we may take different paths over the course of our lives. Some of them may be wildly divergent. Some of them we might not like. Some paths, we may discover, end up being hurtful to ourselves or others. But all of them are made based on the information and desires we had at the time. These paths—some perceived as successes and others as failures, if not outright disasters—all teach us what we want and do not want for our lives. Judging our past choices as good or bad serves to decrease self-confidence and imposes feelings of inadequacy upon us. Learning from our past sets us on a course of living our lives more effectively and efficiently. We all make mistakes. The key is whether we learn from them to improve our lives. Effective and efficient living means we do not keep making the same mistakes over and over again.

The tornado analogy illuminates the folly of using present events to deride past decisions. It is not possible to predict the future, and when the unexpected unravels our plans, it is not productive to beat ourselves up for making those choices. Not making choices or not making plans is not living life. We do the best we are able to overcome the challenges we face. We may make changes along the way, but we keep moving forward.

The tornado analogy is an extreme example of unhealthy time orientation—beating oneself up for past choices because of an unpredicted event that negatively affects one's life. While it may seem absurd to abuse ourselves over not predicting a tornado, many of us allow ourselves to engage in unhealthy time orientation regarding personal relationships, especially "failed" ones. How many of us have, at some point in our lives, lamented our relationship choices by saying, "I should have known better." In doing this, we are reacting like the tornado analogy. We are overlaying a current reality onto the past, when the current reality did not exist. The irritants of today were not present when the choice to commit to the relationship was made. Let us look at an example of an unsuccessful relationship processed from the perspective of the tornado analogy.

Pat and Leslie met in college. Initial attraction and common interests led to sparks, which led to their being inseparable. Love led to marriage and the establishment of a happy home. Years passed with each working hard, but they always made time to spend together. They took frequent trips in their small

SUV, crammed with camping gear, to unwind and experience nature. The distractions of everyday life never seemed much of a concern. They were happiest talking, sharing, and being with each other.

When Leslie was offered a new job, it seemed ideal, with lots of travel and good pay. But the travel started to intrude on their relationship, keeping them apart more than they were together. The camping gear stayed in the garage gathering dust. With Leslie's increasing absence, Pat began to develop a separate life. Pat found new friends to talk to, go to the theater with, and share a growing love of cooking. Nightly phone calls between Leslie and Pat faded to their talking every couple of days. Then the communication dropped to the occasional texts on mundane matters, such as:

"Are you still coming home on the fifteenth?"

"No, got to stay until the eighteenth."

Pat grew to resent Leslie's absence and finally decided enough was enough. It was time to go their separate ways. Leslie offered to stay home more, but to Pat the damage was done. Their lives, once inseparable, had become separate existences. Pat wanted a partner who was available. During the divorce process, Pat thought only about how this had been so predictable. *Sure, Leslie loved to camp, Leslie loved to travel, loved to get away, to get away from everything. Obviously, Leslie would want to get away from me, too. I should have seen this coming. I should have known better. I should have seen who Leslie really was all along.*

In this scenario, Pat is using current resentment of Leslie's frequent travel to reframe memories of the beginning of their relationship. There had been no way then to know Leslie would take a job that would ultimately play a role in separating them. Their relationship was not doomed from the start. Life experiences altered the course of their relationship. The choices they made in the beginning fostered a strong bond. The choices they made over time eroded their bond. Healthier choices would have involved recognizing their relationship was struggling and coming up with a plan of action to address the relationship in its **present** condition. They may have concentrated on better communication, consciously taking more time for one another, and spending more time together. Perhaps engaging in couple's therapy would have been helpful, providing a safe environment to discuss difficult issues. Couple's therapy might have assisted them in recognizing that what they had done in the past was not working for their present relationship.

All of us evolve as we live our lives. Change is an inevitable component of life. Situations change, attitudes change, priorities change, goals change, our bodies change, and the people we are involved with change. It is vital we recognize this and address these changes based on **present** circumstances. This is not to suggest all relationships are worth preserving or are able to be preserved. Despite concerted attempts at reconciliation, not all relationships are salvageable. Some relationships end, some quite acrimoniously. Even if a relationship ends badly, it does not mean the people involved have failed. Instead, the demise of the relationship serves to bring to light what the partners want from this point going forward to live satisfying lives. The relationship's demise does not negate the positive experiences they once had.

Let us look at another example of tornado-analogy thinking. Ann, a young professional woman, reveals that she perceives herself as a terrible, horrible person. I ask her why she thinks this about herself. She shares that when she was 15 years old, she had a baby and gave the child up for adoption. Ann tells me that since she is a successful professional now, she could have provided her baby with a happy, healthy home. Ann's guilt over her perceived abandonment of her child was overwhelming her and preventing her from having a positive self-image. Overlaying her present circumstances of professional success and monetary security onto her past life—when she was a scared, unsure, dependent teen—is classic tornado-analogy thinking. In Ann's case, she is having a tornado in reverse. Instead of everything great being devastated by an unforeseen negative event, Ann's life consisted of earlier overwhelming events that transformed into success and security. Whether the past is good or bad—or the present is good or bad—is irrelevant. What is unhealthy is taking present reality and putting it onto past reality.

It would be more productive for Ann to look back in time to identify her past reality. Her reality was that she was 15 years old, the father of her child was 16 years old, and he wanted nothing to do with her pregnancy. Her parents wanted her to get an abortion, but she refused. The idea of terminating her pregnancy horrified Ann. She was afraid of the challenges of parenting and feared she was ill-prepared to be a good mother. She wanted to finish high school and go to college; she worried that caring for her baby would keep her from fulfilling her academic goals. Most importantly, Ann wanted her baby to have opportunities she believed she was not able to provide. Ann wanted her child to have the best life possible, but she believed that she, by herself, was not ready or able to provide the type of life she wanted for her child.

By identifying the factors that led Ann to give up her child for adoption, she might recognize her past choices were instrumental in making her who she is today. If she had kept her child, Ann might not have been able to go to college or even finish high school. At the time, her educational goals were secondary to concerns about her baby's future. She had little knowledge about how to raise a child, and she did not want her baby to suffer from the many mistakes she feared she would surely make. She wanted the best possible life for her child. Given her circumstances, she did what she thought was best with what she had at the time. If Ann became pregnant today, her decision-making process would be entirely different given her current circumstances. Ann, as a mature adult, is a different person today than she was as a scared, unsupported teenager. Imposing who she is today onto decisions made by who she was in the past is irrational thinking, because who she is now did not exist then.

Ann's current irrationality is leading her to feel inadequate and guilty, and it reduces her self-confidence. Her harsh critique of past decisions causes her to question her decision-making ability, which negatively affects her ability to make healthy choices in the present. Ann will be able to appreciate her ability to make quality decisions now if she recognizes the fallacy of judging her past self by the attributes of her current self. If Ann is able to let go of the negative judgments of her past, and if she is able to understand that she did what she thought was best **at the time** she made her decision, she will be more accepting of her life and who she is today. By living in the past, we impede our ability to live effectively in the present.

Let us look at another example of how the choices we make may lead to perceived failures, but instead reveal paths that allow us to live fuller, more enriched lives. Let us say I am a senior in high school. I am good at math, science, and physics. I do not know what to major in at college. My career counselor suggests majoring in engineering. That makes sense. Engineering uses my talents and strengths. So, I declare a major in engineering my freshman year. I take one semester of engineering courses and I think, *Yuck! I don't like this!* If I process this realization from the perspective of the tornado analogy, I would tell myself, *I should've known better. I shouldn't have tried to major in engineering.*

How do we know about something unless we try it? How else am I supposed to know I do not like engineering without taking courses in it? If I use all the information available when I make a decision, I am more likely to make the best possible choice I know how to at that time. If I make a choice that is intended to be positive for my life, it is all I am able to do. Down the road, I may discover the decision is not what I want. Then I may make changes based on my current desires.

Sometimes we tell ourselves that when we make a choice, we cannot change it. This thinking is erroneous because life is always full of choices. One choice may lead us down a path that presents us with new, unexpected opportunities. These opportunities, in turn, may offer new choices for unexpected paths. This process may lead us far from our original intentions, but it may result in much greater fulfillment and life satisfaction. Some paths may be more difficult or less appealing than had been anticipated. Deciding to leave this path does not mean that you have failed or are a failure. It just means you have learned more about what is important to you and clarified what you desire for your life. How else are you to learn what is important to you unless you try something? Will you make mistakes? Absolutely. If we discover we have made a mistake, we learn from it, apply it to our life **today**, and move forward.

It is good to be aware of our experiences from the past. It is important to apply what we have learned from those experiences to the present. To be healthy, it is crucial to stay present in the present. **We are only able to be effective in the present.** We are unable to change the past. It is only in this moment, at this second, that we are able to take action that affects our lives. If you find yourself in the past, ask yourself this question: *What have I learned from this experience that I may use today?*

## Present Orientation

Years ago, during a college practicum, I worked with people in their final stages of cancer. I observed that there appeared to be two groups of people. One group consisted of individuals who had fully lived their lives. They were successful with rich lives, though not all had money. They had experienced lives full of risks taken and challenges met. They did not always win. They had lost passionate loves. They had experienced grief and heartaches, triumphs and setbacks. They had made mistakes. But they remained courageous and continued to try new things, pursue new experiences, and look to each new day as a new opportunity. Some had made risky choices. They had lost money and made unwise bets. They had failed marriages, and sometimes had less than ideal relationships with those they cared about. They had all made the best choices they knew how to at the time they made them. These choices did not always work out the way they had hoped. In fact, few of them panned out the way they had planned, but they kept going, kept striving, kept learning, and kept moving forward.

This group of people, who had faced life's challenges and were not cowed by setbacks and mistakes, faced the reality of their deaths as they had faced the reality of their lives. They talked openly with family members and sought accurate information from experts and others who had faced similar experiences. They expressed their fears and worries to their families and loved ones, giving them a sense of peace and resolution with their deaths. By being proactive and effective, they were able to die well, with a minimum of death anxiety.

The other group consisted of individuals who struggled in their process of moving toward their deaths. They were full of statements like, "I wish I had...I should have done...If only I had...I was going to...." For me, this group was unsettling to observe. They fought and struggled against the reality they faced. I am convinced these individuals, even if their cancer had gone into complete remission, would still have approached life from the perspective, "I wish I had...." Their lifelong pattern of avoiding risks, not living their lives, fearing making mistakes, and being unwilling to try new things made it more difficult to face the challenges inherent with their deaths. They had excuses or reasons for not doing something that challenged them or necessitated acting outside their normal routines or comfort zones. For example, if they wanted to travel, they would find a multitude of justifications for staying home.

"Airplanes are too crowded."

"What if I miss a connection?"

"It's too expensive right now."

"I don't want to leave my pets."

"I don't speak a foreign language."

"What if terrorists attack?"

"Hotels are too loud."

"I don't trust foreign food."

"What if a storm or earthquake hits?"

"What if I get lost?"

This list of why-nots extinguished any possibility of seeing new places and pursuing new ideas or dreams. If these individuals considered starting a business, they would tell themselves a multitude of reasons not to pursue it. There were always too many risks to try out their ideas. The same would be true for activities. It would be too dangerous to climb a mountain, camp in the woods, or go skiing, much less scuba dive or skydive.

They never tried most of the dreams, hopes, aspirations, and activities they wanted to.

Because of their lifelong avoidance of challenges, they struggled to communicate with their partners and loved ones about their deaths, their final wishes, and their aspirations for how their families would continue without them. Some would not even discuss their funeral arrangements, or whether they wanted to be buried or cremated. They avoided addressing critical business matters. Their inability to confront these challenges created an atmosphere of anxiety, tension, and uncertainty for everyone involved. These people could not find a sense of peace and resolution with their deaths. By avoiding the reality of death and being ineffective in addressing their experience with themselves and others, they were unable to die well and experienced heightened death anxiety.

In working with these two groups of people, I learned an invaluable gem of knowledge: The only time we have in life is this moment, this second. The only time we may live our lives effectively is this moment, this second. That is why it is so important to live in the present. To live a full, complete life it is necessary to stay in the present. Being in this moment, this second, allows us to experience the moments in time that, when put together, build life experiences.

To clarify, living in the future or in the past is **not** life experience. Ruminating on the future or the past involves thought, not action, and thus denies me life experiences. If I am living in the future or the past, I am living in my head and am not really present. If I want something to be different in my life, there is no place for change to occur unless I make that change in the present. Once I am in the present, I may make choices to move and alter my life in another direction. Without being present, it is impossible to alter or change my life. Being present allows me to consciously appreciate events occurring in my life and feel emotions elicited by these experiences. Being present ultimately leads me to feeling more alive.

Another advantage of living in the present is that we are able to shed our experiences of the past. We are able to cut the ties and threads to the past that anchor us and make it difficult to be in the present. Consider people who are struggling to let go of bad habits or behavior. They may drink too much or eat unhealthily. Or perhaps they engage in hurtful behaviors toward others, such as cheating on partners or taking advantage of family members and friends. Maybe their style of relating to others does not serve them well. Others may find them abrasive, sarcastic, withdrawn, or passive-aggressive. Change occurs by making different choices in the present. If these people desire to improve their lives and their relationships, change is only possible through actions and choices they make in the present. Excuses such as, "This is just how I am," or "I'm like this because...," are instances of allowing the past to dictate current choices. By focusing on present choices and living in the present, individuals may create a new and different reality for themselves. Without focusing on the present, the past may easily drag people down, leading them to ruminate on inadequacies of the past rather than creating a new way of living.

Another way to think about the present and its ability for change are instances when we have had difficult and painful past experiences. In these instances, it is sometimes helpful to share and to talk through what has happened. However, staying in the past, ruminating about these instances, is not productive. The healthier way to process these situations is to ask ourselves, *How am I affected today by this experience?*

It is not possible to go back and change those painful experiences. However, in the present we may reframe and cope with the impact of the painful experience. Since we are unable to change the past, it is only effective to focus on the present. By focusing on the present, we are able to identify ways to change so we are no longer affected by those negative past experiences. We are likely to be more effective in addressing past negative experiences if we apply coping strategies today. By changing the way we process our lives in the present, such as reframing the effects of difficult past experiences, we gain efficiency and effectiveness in our lives.

## THE PRESENT AND THE CAKE ANALOGY

As we live in the present, it is beneficial to consider **how** we do so. Many of us tell ourselves we are supposed to perform all sorts of tasks at the same time. Some people call this "multitasking." While some are good at multitasking, simultaneously moving from one task to the other without tripping, multitasking threatens most people's ability to be present. It may throw us into functioning on automatic pilot or jumping into the future.

Trying to do everything at once may lead us to feel overwhelmed and out of control.

Consider the cake analogy. If I try to stuff an entire cake into my mouth all at once, I will choke. There is no way I may chew and swallow an entire cake at once, let alone get the whole thing into my mouth. However, if I cut the cake into pieces, I may eat a piece at a time. I may decide to put some pieces in the freezer and pull them out at a time that better suits me for eating, or I may eat the entire cake at once, one piece at a time. This analogy demonstrates that we may choose when and how we eat the cake, piece by piece. It allows us to determine what to do with each piece.

It is important to keep in mind that if we are completing multiple tasks, it is for us to determine how many to complete, in what order they are completed, when they are completed, and so on. We must be careful when multitasking or expecting ourselves to complete numerous tasks at once, as our ability to be present may be impeded. If I place expectations on myself to do multiple tasks at once, I run the risk of feeling like the tasks I expect of myself—or that others expect me to complete—are coming from an external locus of control. This external locus of control will lead to feeling ineffective and create stress. It is best to take it one thing at a time, even if that involves doing multiple "one-thing-at-a-time" tasks in succession.

## THE BRICK ANALOGY AND CHANGE

Remember, living in the present allows us to make change today that is consistent with what we want tomorrow. Wishing something to be different is not enough. Consider this analogy. If there is a pile of bricks on one side of the room and I want them on the other side, just wishing them to be moved is not effective. I may wish those bricks to the other side of the room all I want, but that is not going to move them. However, if I pick up one brick, carry it to the other side of the room, put it down, and repeat the process, I will eventually move the entire pile—one brick at a time. At the point I moved the first brick, there was a conscious choice to make change. Even though one brick may not seem like much, especially if the pile of bricks is large, it is a step toward meeting my goal. I may move all the bricks at once, I may move one brick a day, or I may move one brick a year. The key is that moving the bricks signifies change.

The brick analogy reminds us of the importance of living in the present to live and experience our lives. Living in the present allows us to live as effectively as possible. This, in turn, leads to fulfillment and satisfaction. In this way, we are able to break the chains of the past. Living in the present allows us to invest in our future.

If I want to lose weight, every pound shed is a brick moved. If I want a college degree, every class I attend is a brick moved. If I want to reduce my drinking, every sober day is a brick moved. If I want to stop cheating or taking advantage of people, being less deceptive and more honest is a brick moved. If I want to be less abrasive, every time I encourage rather than disparage is a brick moved. If I want something to be different in my life, it is necessary for me to make a conscious choice to take action to make it different.

Once I am in the present, I am able to make choices to alter my life. Without being in the present, it is impossible to alter or change my life. As stated above, the brick analogy teaches us that small steps may result in significant change. Change, however, is not exclusively constructive. Change may also be destructive. Just as we are able to make choices to improve our lives, our choices may also damage our lives. Bad food choices may be bricks toward obesity and poor health. Alcoholic drinks may be bricks on the path to alcoholism. Infidelity may be bricks toward the dissolution of a relationship. Some of our choices may undermine our stated goals of living healthier, fulfilling lives. The present offers us decisions. Our choices may be productive or counterproductive toward our goals. Choice is precisely that: choice. We may choose to live our lives well or not. We have the freedom to live our lives constructively. We have the freedom to live our lives destructively. It is **our** choice.

A single misstep does not undo all the constructive work we have done before or prevent us from moving forward from that point on. If our weight loss goal is undermined by a few gained pounds, it does not mean we give up on our goal. It simply means there is a little more work to do than before. We have simply taken a few bricks away from our goal pile, and it is necessary to pick them up again and carry them back. Not all goals are met with a straight path. Many missteps and detours may deflect us along the way. While they may aggravate us, when used constructively, missteps alert us to where we might best focus our attention. They may motivate us further toward meeting our goal.

Along the path to weight loss, eating an entire bag of cookies may fill us with feelings of guilt and self-loathing. These feelings might be so intense that they discourage us or cause us to quit our weight-loss goal. Rather than beating ourselves up over momentary weakness in the face of chocolate, a constructive response to our bloated belly is to identify our behavior, recognize it, and change it. If we struggle to resist the temptation within arm's reach, it may be better to avoid bringing cookies into the house for a while. To eat or not eat the cookie is not the question—it is the choice. Some choices are easier to make than others. If you find yourself struggling to make constructive choices, it may be better to alter your environment so it is easier to make better decisions. In this case, not having cookies in the house makes it easier to not scarf down an entire bag of rich, sweet, chocolaty, chewy, yummy cookies.

# Self-Reflection

Ask yourself whether you are living in the past, the present, or the future. If you are living in the future, ask yourself, *What may I do today to make my tomorrow what I want it to be?* Think about two things you want for your future. When you identify them, use the brick analogy to determine if you are actually moving bricks to make your future what you want it to be, or if you are merely wishing the bricks would be on the other side of the room. Our future goals are only met by actively taking steps to make them a reality. We achieve goals by actively making constructive choices in the present to fulfill them.

If you are living in the past, ask yourself, *What have I learned from my past experiences that I may use today, so I do not make the same mistake twice?* You may want to spend some time writing down what you have learned from your experiences that you may use today. Think about two instances where you have used the tornado analogy. In other words, think of two instances where you have looked back on your life and thought, *I should have this...I should not have that....* Whenever you look back and think, *should have* or *should not have*, it is a red flag that you are engaging in tornado-analogy thinking. As you become aware of these instances, look into the past to identify what was actually occurring at that point in time that led you to make the choice you made. Let go of the negative, self-punitive aspects of tornado-analogy thinking that undermines your self-confidence. Identify and reframe your thoughts by specifying what you learned from that experience that you may use today. This reframing is how we separate ourselves from the past, so we may make different choices for our lives and develop healthier coping skills today. It will allow you to more effectively face life's challenges.

If you want to stop an unhealthy habit or desire to change an aspect of your life, identify ways you may alter your behavior today. Change is only possible if you make a conscious choice—this moment, this second—to do something differently. As you make the choice to behave differently, your self-confidence will grow and you will find yourself feeling more effective and efficient in changing habits or aspects of your life.

If you have painful and difficult past experiences, it may be beneficial to process those events with a trusted friend or therapist. However, ruminating about the past is not constructive. Instead, the best way to move beyond these difficult experiences is to ask yourself how they affect you today. Your ability to change is only in the present.

If you are living in the present, that is absolutely fabulous! Keep it up! If you are living in the future or the past, practice ways to live in the present. It is only in the present that we are able to effectively achieve life satisfaction.

# PRINCIPLE III

## Developing a Positive Relationship with Myself

# CHAPTER 4

---

# My Internal Dialogue

## What is Internal Dialogue?

We are always talking to ourselves. Our internal dialogue is powerful in creating our internal reality. It denotes the nature of our relationship with ourselves. We may describe the nature of our internal dialogue as positive, supportive, loving, and kind. We may also describe it as critical, demeaning, hateful, and unkind. Or, we may describe it in shades between these extremes. The nature of our internal dialogue represents the nature of the relationship we have with ourselves.

Some of us are totally internal in our dialogue. Others may observe that their dialogue is sometimes external. In other words, some of us occasionally talk out loud to ourselves. By this, I do not mean people are carrying on entire conversations with themselves or incessantly muttering. Instead, I mean people who occasionally—usually when confronted with a stressful or complex situation—verbally express their thought process as a way to clarify their course of action or direct themselves.

We may not be consciously aware of it, but if we stop and observe our thought processes, we may begin to identify our internal dialogue constantly giving ourselves messages. The messages may be critical about our performance. We may talk to ourselves about our failure to reach perfection, what we have done wrong, how we may have done something differently, or how we may have embarrassed ourselves in some way. On the other hand, the messages may be encouraging and supportive. We may tell ourselves we did a good job, that we are doing the right thing, or that we are on the right path toward meeting a goal.

For myself, dialogue is sometimes internal and external. If I am focusing on a complicated or stressful task, I verbally talk myself through it. When I am preparing to depart for an out-of-town presentation, I go through a list of things to gather, out loud, to ensure I am taking care of all the necessary details. I say to myself, "I emailed the presentation slides to the conference director. I have my backup flash drive in my briefcase. I have the handouts, my notes in braille, and my notes in print. I have my braille computer. I have my white cane as an alternate form of mobility, I have Diaz's dog food, his portable water dish, and his guide dog ID card. I'm good to go."

I do this to remind myself to bring all the necessary things that cannot be replaced when I arrive. I do not worry about forgetting a toothbrush or an article of clothing because if I forget them, I am able to buy replacements later. I am aware that my external dialogue heightens my awareness and ensures

I have addressed the crucial components of my presentation and my travel requirements.

I have noticed that as my available vision declines, I find it useful at times to direct myself with external dialogue. If I am struggling to locate my cellphone, a reminder note, or the stapler, I will ask myself out loud, "Okay, where did I have it last? Was it in my office? Did I leave it on the reception desk? Did I leave it on top of the file cabinet?" By talking myself through a search, I avoid wasting time pawing around, trying to find something I have difficulty seeing until I am right on top of it. Through the use of external dialogue, I clear my mind of other thoughts and am able to more clearly focus on the main problem at hand. Using external dialogue helps me prioritize my thoughts and direct my actions, but it may be distracting to others nearby. I often declare, "Nothing, just talking to myself as usual," to staff within earshot who call out, "What, Cheryl?"

Consider the nature of your own internal dialogue. How would you describe how you relate with yourself? Are you positive and supportive, or are you critical and demeaning? Let me give you an example. Suppose I burn dinner. That scenario is easily within the realm of possibility, because I am often quickly absorbed by other tasks when taking advantage of a free moment. When the all-too-frequent charring occurs and I have a pan of stove-top briquettes, am I thinking, *You stupid little idiot, look what you just did,* or am I thinking, *Cheryl, get rid of this burned food and decide what else to do for dinner. It would be better to pay more attention to what you are doing while you are cooking.*

From this example, we see we are able to relate with ourselves in a manner that is critical and demeaning, or in a manner that is positive and supportive. It is important for each of us to reflect on the nature of our relationship with ourselves. We will find in examining the nature of our internal dialogue that the manner in which we relate with ourselves is a conscious choice. Whether we are supportive or demeaning to ourselves is up to us.

# Discovering the Origins of Internal Dialogue

The following question is not intended to be blaming or accusatory. It is intended to illuminate a psychological concept that may explain why you engage in the type of internal dialogue you do. The question is this: Who, in your entire life, does your internal dialogue most sound like?

The majority of us will say their internal dialogue most resembles a primary caregiver while they were growing up. Usually, it is their mom, dad, grandma, grandpa, aunt, uncle, older sibling, or whoever was primarily responsible for raising them. I ask this question to demonstrate a psychological concept called vicarious learning, or model learning. Because our brains are so effective and efficient, we are able to learn from observation. It may be that the person we learned from was negative toward themselves, toward their world, toward others, and perhaps, toward us while we were growing up. Again, addressing this is not intended to be blaming or accusatory, but to assist in understanding how we learn to interact with ourselves and others.

Clients frequently ask, "Cheryl, why am I so negative toward myself?" If they perceive themselves as experiencing negative internal dialogue, I explain to them that they may have learned negative internal dialogue through experiences while growing up. I go on to inform them that this does not involve complex psychological dynamics. Instead, it involves years of learned behavior. For example, if I observed my primary caregiver being perfectionistic and critical of herself, perfectionistic and critical of her interactions with others, and perhaps directing perfectionistic or critical messages toward me, I may learn to relate with myself in a similar manner. In addition, if my personality tends to be naturally perfectionistic or critical, I am even more likely to be negative and critical toward myself.

Let us look at a few examples of who your primary caregivers may have been and how their ways of approaching their world may have impacted the development of your own internal dialogue.

If you grew up with Dad swearing unholy tirades at traffic, throwing his shoes at the wall during football games, chucking tools when the mower would not start, and yelling at you when you were talking during his shows, you may have learned that your first impulse or reaction when you get frustrated is to fly into a rage.

If Mom was near the top of her grad school class, was the youngest executive at her firm, always had your schedule planned, always got you where you needed to be when you needed to be there, then you may have learned to desire control, to be highly organized, and to avoid being tardy. You may be uncomfortable when there is not a plan.

If Aunt Latisha never left the house without her "face" on, her makeup perfect, her clothes neatly pressed and immaculate, and every hair in place, you may have learned to be hesitant to go outside unless you look your best. You might always fret about your appearance.

If Grandma Mimi always had a hot meal cooking and a tin of cookies at the ready, or was always quick to give a warm hug, an encouraging word, and a sympathetic ear, you may have learned to be prone to meet the needs of others before your own.

If Uncle Juan was critical of others, finding fault with every-thing, lamenting how everything was going to hell, you may have learned to overlook the positives in people and new circumstances. You may only focus on and look for all that is negative.

If Grandpa Joe went around whistling cheery tunes, never met a stranger he did not like, and treated each day like a precious gift, you may have learned to be eager to meet new people, finding the good in everyone and everything.

If your stepmom did not see the point in traveling, did not dare leave her job even though she hated it, avoided speaking up for herself, and always had an excuse not to go to a party or other gatherings, you may have learned to be fearful of change, new people, and new circumstances. You may have learned to be hesitant to pursue new opportunities.

If your stepdad seldom left the couch unless it was to grab another beer, wore the same old tattered clothes, never fixed anything until it broke off in his hand, and saw no point in caring what others thought or said about him, you may have learned to be less motivated to improve yourself, your relationships, or your circumstances.

One or more of our primary caregivers may have played a significant role in the development of the nature of our internal dialogue. What we vicariously learned from our primary care-givers is filtered through our personality. Our personality may work in opposition to what we have vicariously learned, or it may exacerbate what we have learned.

For example, if a timid and shy person grows up with an angry father, their internal dialogue might reflect wanting to avoid people who exhibit anger. If a person who is highly energetic and extroverted grows up with a stepmother who is fearful of experiencing the world, their internal dialogue might reflect a heightened desire for adventure to avoid missing out on new experiences. If a procrastinator grows up with a couch potato stepfather, their internal dialogue may discourage them from wanting to improve their lives or set goals. It may encourage them to find ways to avoid the responsibility of supporting themselves. If a people-pleaser grows up with a grandmother who is a nurturer, their internal dialogue may urge them to focus on the needs of others, perhaps to the neglect of their own desires.

Our first response is quite often to follow what we have vicariously learned and react in a similar manner. However, our personalities may drive us to act in an opposite manner from what we grew up observing. Regardless of whether we mimic or rebuke behaviors exhibited by our primary caregivers, we are never locked into being a product of our environment. Once we recognize the nature of our internal dialogue and where it comes from, we are able to make the conscious choice to change it. Changing our internal dialogue is a significant step toward becoming who we want to be.

# The Power of Internal Dialogue

To understand the power of internal dialogue, it is important to understand two concepts in psychology: self-fulfilling prophecy and covert rehearsal. Let us look at each of these.

## SELF-FULFILLING PROPHECY

Self-fulfilling prophecy is the idea that someone will behave in a manner consistent with what they have been told about themselves by others or their own self-perceptions, whether the perceptions are accurate or inaccurate. These messages may originate from a person receiving direct messages, erroneously perceiving messages, and receiving messages from societal expectations.

Suppose a child is told he is ugly, unattractive, and stupid, or is given other negative messages. He is likely to believe them.

These messages may have greater impact if they come from significant individuals in his life, such as his parents, siblings, teachers, coaches, and peers. These messages may heavily influence the development of the child's internal dialogue and eventually impact his behavior.

It is not necessary for these messages to be blatant. Sometimes they are much more subtle, embedded in the family atmosphere and erroneously perceived by the child. Suppose a young girl is working on a math assignment. She gets stuck on a problem and seeks help from her mother. Mom may say, totally innocently, "Honey, I've never really been good at math. Dad is great at it, so when he comes home, why don't you ask him to help you?" There is nothing wrong with what Mom said to her daughter. However, her daughter may erroneously perceive her mother's statement. She may think, *I want to be like Mom. Girls don't do math—boys do.*

Mom's explanation may be totally misconstrued by her daughter. She may erroneously internalize an unintended message: Girls don't do math—boys do. From the little girl's perspective, she may also be quick to think this because of the societal norm at her school, where all the math and science teachers are men. Then there are the science shows she watches, which feature mostly male presenters.

Suppose a little girl has been told women do not become doctors, but nurses. Women do not become business leaders, but secretaries. Women are to be teachers, not engineers. A girl may certainly wish upon a star, but she should not waste her time studying them or dreaming of being an astronaut. A good girl should look to being a good wife and mother. Over time, these messages may become the little girl's beliefs. These are all examples of societal messages a little girl may receive. Many of us are likely to make choices consistent with what we have been told or perceive.

The little girl also may have acquired messages that she is inadequate, she is not doing very well, and she is not meeting expectations. At first, when she hears these messages, it stings. She may become sad and even cry. But if she hears these negative messages over and over again, they may not sting as much because, in her perception, they are becoming her reality. Once she internalizes the negative messages, she may repeat them over and over to herself. I envision it as being a wheel that turns. Every time she thinks about these negative messages, they are reinforced and the wheel spins faster and faster, with the negative messages becoming stronger and stronger. Then, as she moves through life, she may make choices that are consistent with the negative messages and support, validate, and even further reinforce them. Her choices and behaviors that validate the negative messages are the self-fulfilling prophecy.

We are going to now look at the concept of covert rehearsal, but we will come back to the concept of self-fulfilling prophecy in just a moment.

## COVERT REHEARSAL

When we talk about rehearsal, we are talking about practice. There is covert (internal) and overt (external) rehearsal. The concept of covert rehearsal is becoming much more understood in the literature around visualization. It is used in many areas, including athletics. A coach or sports psychologist might encourage an athlete to internally focus and visualize what they want to do. Take, for example, a skier who is preparing for a competition. The coach may encourage him to absorb as much information about the course as possible while practicing on the slope. After practice, the coach asks him to rehearse and recreate his experience in his mind in as much detail as possible. This visualization creates an internal map. This mental foundation will allow the skier to anticipate the demands of the course, even if the snow conditions significantly change during the competition. No matter the actual conditions of the course, the pre-race mental map serves as a foundation for how he will approach the course during competition.

Another example is a figure skater or a gymnast who is instructed to achieve a nice, relaxed state. The coach might turn on the music of her routine and ask her to visualize herself performing it flawlessly. If the athlete finds it difficult to see herself performing perfectly, she will overtly practice the sections she is having difficulty visualizing. Again, the idea is for the athlete to perform according to what she has rehearsed in her mind.

Musicians also use mental rehearsal to prepare for performances. Without playing their instrument, they listen to their performance, note for note, in their mind. If a concert pianist is preparing for a concert and discovers gaps or flaws in the mental rehearsal of her pieces, she will overtly rehearse the problem section on the piano. The purpose is to fill in the gaps in her mental rendition of the piece.

Covert rehearsal compels the mind and body to perform in a desired manner, regardless of the stressors, distractions, and conditions during the actual performance, routine, or race. It assists a performer in achieving higher degrees of perfection, because their actions are all but reflexive. It also serves to reduce stress and performance anxiety because the mind and body are prepared and focused.

What we say to ourselves over and over again in our internal dialogue is a form of covert rehearsal. Similar to a performer's covert rehearsal, perceptions of ourselves become embedded—like a routine—through our internal dialogue. The perception becomes automatic with each rehearsal. If I struggled with my first math class and went on to tell myself over and over again that I am not good at math, I am likely to deduce I have no abilities with anything math-related. Because of my internal dialogue disparaging my math abilities, I automatically assume I will not have any success with, or understanding of, chemistry, physics, astronomy, engineering, accounting, or computer science. By taking one negative experience and compounding it with incessant negative internal dialogue, I have effectively cut myself off from all sorts of potentially rewarding and interesting fields of study. Our internal dialogue is very powerful and compels us to think or act in a particular way. Changing our way of thinking or acting will be very difficult unless we first change our internal dialogue.

Now that we understand how covert rehearsal influences internal dialogue, let us look at how internal dialogue manifests into self-fulfilling prophecy.

# Internal Dialogue and Self-Fulfilling Prophecy

Here are four scenarios of how a young woman's internal dialogue may affect her dating behaviors and choices.

In the first scenario, the young woman's internal dialogue tells her she is unattractive, unintelligent, unworthy, incapable, and so on. If her partner treats her poorly, what is she likely to do? Her response may be to accept this treatment because the messages are familiar and consistent with her self-messages of worthlessness and not deserving to be treated well.

In the second scenario, the young woman's internal dialogue tells her she is attractive, intelligent, competent, worthy, and so on. If her partner treats her poorly, what is she likely to do? Her response may be to end the relationship because his messages are unfamiliar and inconsistent with her self-messages of worthiness and deserving to be treated well.

In the third scenario, let us look once again at the young woman feeling negatively about herself. If her partner treats her well, what is she likely to do? There may be two possible outcomes. The first possibility is she may sabotage the relationship. Her partner treating her well is inconsistent with her self-messages of worthlessness. This inconsistency is likely to create anxiety for her, and it may be more comfortable for her to stop pursuing the relationship or sabotage it. She may not show up for dates or she may cheat on her partner to increase the likelihood her partner will end the relationship, thus reinforcing her feelings of unworthiness.

The second possibility is, despite her negative internal dialogue, she recalls times in the past when she received encouragement, support, and compliments on her abilities from friends, teachers, coaches, some family members, and others. This remembrance, combined with the validation from her partner, may lead her to question her negative internal dialogue. Her way of coping with the conflict between what she tells herself and what she is told by others may encourage her to split from her negative self-perception. In other words, she may learn to present herself in a manner consistent with the positive messages she receives from others. She may learn to present herself as competent, intelligent, capable, and so on. However, if you were to ask this young woman how she feels about herself and her abilities, her perception of herself may be incongruent with her presentation to others. She may continue to perceive herself as inadequate. She will feel as though she is an impostor, pretending to be something that, deep down, she feels she is not.

In the fourth scenario, the young woman who feels positively about herself finds a partner who treats her well. This relationship has a higher likelihood of success because her partner's actions are consistent with her perception that she is worthy of being treated well.

Our internal dialogue plays a crucial role in how we perceive ourselves and our world. If we seek to change and improve our internal dialogue, it is vital we understand the nature of that internal dialogue. Being aware of how we have developed our internal dialogue will provide us with insight in understanding its nature. It is important to be aware that our internal dialogue has been rehearsed for as many years as we are old. To improve our internal dialogue, it will be necessary to overtly and covertly rehearse changes. This rehearsal is often a challenging process and requires frequent and consistent attention. However, with sincere effort and conscious choice, it is possible to transform your internal dialogue—and therefore, your relationship with yourself—into something loving, kind, and supportive. The next chapter presents skills and strategies for changing your internal dialogue.

# Self-Reflection

Observe your dialogue. Do you talk with yourself internally, or do you talk out loud to yourself? Or is your dialogue a combination of the two? One way is not better than the other. Recognizing how you relate with yourself will assist you in understanding how you function with your dialogue.

Consider how your internal dialogue is affecting your life choices. Take time to consider the following questions and be willing to honestly reflect on your answers. I encourage you to not be blaming or accusatory. Recognize your answers and know you are able to change them.

- What are the messages I am giving myself?
- Where did I get these messages?
- How do I perceive myself?
- Do I give myself positive messages, or am I critical and demeaning?
- Am I supportive of myself in my endeavors?
- Do I encourage myself during times of stress?

Of course, the same questions may be presented from a less positive light.

- Am I being critical of myself?
- Am I being demeaning of myself?
- Am I being discouraging and critical in the manner I approach myself and while completing tasks?
- Do I tell myself I am incapable of performing tasks before I even start them?
- Do negative messages keep me from pursuing opportunities I would like to pursue?

Taking time to honestly evaluate your answers may assist you in identifying the nature of your relationship with yourself. If you discover you are particularly negative toward yourself, you may change your internal dialogue by learning, developing, and implementing the skills and strategies presented in the next chapter.

# CHAPTER 5

---

# Countering Negative Internal Dialogue

This chapter explores three strategies that are effective in changing negative internal dialogue into positive internal dialogue. They are thought-stopping, the child analogy of internal dialogue, and the Five Rs. You may find yourself gravitating to one strategy more than another, based on how you relate to each strategy. Each comes from a unique perspective, and you may find one that works especially well for you. I encourage you to find the strategy or combination of strategies that work best for you. Whatever strategy you decide to use it is best to apply it consistently for it to be effective.

## Thought-Stopping

Thought-stopping is a coping strategy and a valuable technique to counter and change negative internal dialogue. It involves identifying negative internal dialogue and stopping it. However, simply stopping it is not enough. The key is to replace negative internal dialogue with positive, supportive statements. To be effective, it is necessary for these supportive statements to be grounded in reality.

For a negative self-message to become strong, it must be rehearsed and reinforced. As I rehearse and practice my negative internal dialogue, it is reinforced to the point it becomes automatic. Thought-stopping follows the same logic. Suppose I leave a glass of water on the kitchen counter. Given my limited vision, I might forget about it and knock the glass over the next time I go into the kitchen. My initial internal dialogue may exclaim, *Cheryl, how stupid! How clumsy!* If I am engaging in very negative internal dialogue, it might sound something like, *What an idiot I am! How could I be so stupid?*

Negative thought processes and negative internal dialogue are like a wheel spinning clockwise. Thought-stopping throws a wrench in the spokes of the spinning wheel of negativity. At best, it only stops the wheel. Many people assume the strategy of thought-stopping is complete with only stopping the thought. It is imperative, however, to replace the negative thought with positive internal dialogue once it is stopped. We want to make the wheel turn in the opposite direction. This is accomplished by replacing negative internal dialogue with realistic, encouraging, and positive internal messages. Rehearsed over and over again, these positive self-messages create a more positive internal dialogue, which with consistent practice over time, will become more automatic.

Let us look again at my spilled glass of water. The moment I become aware of saying something negative to myself like, *How stupid! How clumsy!*, I will tell myself, *Stop,* to put a wrench in my spinning wheel of negativity. If I am by myself, I may say, "Stop," out loud, using external dialogue to emphasize my deliberate change in thinking. If I am with other people, I will internally say, *Stop,* because I do not want to be distracted by someone asking, "Stop what?," or have other people cock their heads and wonder, *What's going on with Cheryl today?* Thought-stopping is the first step. I will then replace my negative self-message with messages that are supportive and encouraging, but do not deny reality. I might say to myself, *Cheryl, it's a mess and it's inconvenient, but it's not a big deal. Fill your glass and this time when you put it on the counter, be more aware of where you put it.*

To successfully change negative internal dialogue, it is critical to replace it with realistic, positive internal dialogue. Attempting to counter, *I suck at my job,* with, *I'm the best employee they've got,* will not be very effective in countering negative internal dialogue if it is not based in reality. The agenda is not to lie to ourselves. If I tell myself I am the best employee, and I clearly know that is not true because there are others who have more experience and more expertise, the excessive positive self-messages will not be effective because I know I am trying to fool myself. Instead, countering with, *I do a good job. I feel good about the work I do. I'm always willing to learn new tasks. I'm here on time*, will help replace negative internal dialogue with realistic positive internal dialogue. The goal is not to throw out willy-nilly positive, cheery statements, but to give ourselves messages that are consistent with our lives and who we are. In other words, it is important to consider what I am telling myself, as though I am having a dialogue with myself, rather than mindlessly and automatically replacing what I am saying with something positive.

Many people tell me that when they look in the mirror, they say to themselves something like, *Yuck, I'm fat!* Using the word "fat" is a negative judgment about their weight. *I've not been exercising and I'm gaining weight,* would be a reality-based statement without judgment. After telling themselves, *Stop*, following their negative "fat" assessment, they would be better served by replacing this negative internal dialogue with, *I know I've not been eating well lately. I've not been exercising like I usually do. I'm going to start addressing this right now. I'm going to eat better today, and I'll get back to exercising right away. I'll look and feel better soon*. These statements accept the reality of their change in appearance and provide positive ways to think about themselves. These messages also provide supportive encouragement to move forward to make change.

Now, consider instances of your own negative internal dialogue. Reframe and rehearse how you might approach yourself differently in situations in which you have been, or are currently using, negative internal dialogue. If you practice how you would compose your internal dialogue differently in situations you have already experienced, you will be more capable of responding in a healthier manner when similar situations arise. I strongly encourage you to take time to think about instances of negative internal dialogue. Then, identify how you would use thought-stopping and replace the negative self-messages with positive, supportive internal dialogue that does not deny reality.

When people first attempt this process, they may struggle to come up with positive and supportive internal dialogue. This is especially true for people who have allowed years of negative internal dialogue to become ingrained to the point it is an automatic response. While developing the thought-stopping technique, it is important to understand you have rehearsed and practiced your internal dialogue for as many years as you are old. Combatting entrenched negativity with positive and supportive internal dialogue may be very much like learning how to walk.

Consider the trials of a baby. A baby does not go from lying helpless on the floor to tearing through the house in a single afternoon, day, or week. It is a process that takes time and a considerable number of bumps and tumbles. She learns to roll onto her tummy, which evolves into attempts to crawl, jerking forward and backward. Then there are wobbly attempts to pull herself while grasping at anything within reach, whether it is a chair, a couch, a pant leg, the dog, or a precariously stacked pile of books. She is likely to fall on her bottom repeatedly. She may cry in frustration. But with determination, she will get back up and continue trying, over and over again. With encouragement—or even on her own—she will eventually take a few tentative steps. Then the refining process begins. Over time, she goes from ambling into walls, family members, and pets to running through the house. Tears, bumps, and bruises are part of the process. Learning to walk never goes straight from a desire to get around to walking with a solid, steady gait without a great deal of missteps and tumbles along the way.

You may experience similar feelings as you transform your internal dialogue. You may grow frustrated. At times, you may feel like crying. Some days you may feel like you are striding along. Other days, you may be smacking into everything around you. But improvement is a process. It takes time. It takes practice. Reassure yourself. Encourage yourself. Support yourself. Do not give up. It may take a while. And remember, even the most experienced walker trips now and then.

Some people describe the process of changing internal dialogue as having an angel and a devil perched on either shoulder. On one shoulder, the angel provides support and encouragement, reframing negative self-statements. On the other shoulder, the devil whispers a steady stream of negativity. Using thought-stopping, the angel assures them, "Stop! Don't give in to the negativity. You are able to do this. Don't give up. Take one step at a time. Move one brick at a time. This will get better and better." This surge of optimism is often dampened by the scowling devil, who scolds them, "Don't believe all this psychobabble crap! It's just a ploy to sell books! You know you're never going to change. Let's go get some ice cream and pig out."

If you struggle with this sort of internal conflict, take the time to have a very frank conversation with yourself. That conversation may go something like, *Negative self, I am choosing to no longer give you any energy. I am choosing not to be negative with myself. It does me no good. I am choosing to be positive and supportive with myself. I am no longer going to listen to these negative statements, and I will no longer give them any power or energy.* This conversation highlights the impact our energy and attitude have on our internal dialogue. If we give our energy to negative thoughts, they will grow bigger and become automatic. If we give our energy to positive thoughts, they will grow bigger and become automatic. Making the conscious choice to feed positive messages to yourself and consciously stop negative naysaying will enable you to construct and reinforce positive internal dialogue that, over time, will become more automatic.

# The Child Analogy of Internal Dialogue

Sometimes, because negativity is so ingrained and automatic, we do not know what to say to ourselves once we have identified negative internal dialogue. This makes it difficult to come up with a positive replacement statement. The child analogy offers the opportunity to consider how you are able to use positive internal dialogue to replace negative internal dialogue from a more personal perspective.

Suppose you are sitting on a bench at a local park. It is a beautiful day and you are enjoying the sunshine. There are many children running around having fun. You recognize your neighbor's child among the whirling, squealing pack, but there is no sign of either of her parents. She spots you, gives you a quick wave, and shouts hello. She continues chasing her friends. Out of the corner of your eye, you catch a glimpse of her falling on a patch of pavement. She begins to wail. After she gets to her feet, she hobbles toward you, stumbling in her flip-flops, crying with a badly scraped knee. What are you going to do for her?

Most people say they are going to help her. They will reassure her by telling her she is okay and offer her a tissue to wipe away her tears. They might find a nearby restroom to clean up her scraped knee. Perhaps they will call her parents and offer to take her home.

Most people say they would not hesitate to take care of this little girl. They would take care of her emotionally by reassuring her. They would care for her physically by helping her clean up her scraped knee. Not all people would mention their concerns to the little girl about the pitfalls of running in flip-flops. However, it is appropriate to address the reality of how her choice of running in flip-flops may have contributed to her getting hurt. **How** we say this to her is key. If we communicate our concerns about how she might play more safely in a positive and supportive manner, she is much more likely to receive this message in the manner it is intended: We are concerned for her safety and do not want to see her hurt again.

There are many ways to communicate our concern in a positive way. We may say, "Dear, it's not a good idea to run in flip-flops. It's much easier to trip and fall. If you want to run, tennis shoes are a better choice. If you don't have your tennies, then stick to the grass because if you fall, it probably won't hurt as badly." By being supportive when teaching the little girl about the realities of her situation, she is much more likely to understand and appreciate the message. By being negative, accusatory, or judgmental, she is likely to take away a variety of unintended and harmful messages. We may address the reality of the situation in a positive, supportive manner that enhances the opportunity for constructive learning. If we lash out in a critical and punitive manner, it will only serve to intimidate rather than educate the little girl.

Let us look at another scenario that further demonstrates this idea. Suppose you are at a store and hear, *SPLAT,* followed by the piercing wail of a young boy after he falls out of a shopping cart. As you turn around, you see a woman grab her son by the wrist and yank him from the floor, swatting his behind. She shrieks, "You stupid little idiot! I told you not to do that! I told you you'd fall! It's your own fault!" Most of us would be horrified to see and hear a child being treated this way. Not only is this very unkind to the boy, he is also likely to receive three potent negative messages:

1. *I'm a stupid little idiot.*

2. *It's my own fault I'm hurting.*

3. *If I'm hurting, don't go to Mom because she'll just yell at me and spank me.*

There are many constructive ways to address realities in our lives. The mother of the boy in the store did not consider the negative messages she was giving her son. The least she might have done was ask if he was okay. That question would have given him the clear message that she cares about him. She then might have addressed the reality of falling out of the shopping cart as a learning opportunity by explaining this was the reason she had asked him not to hang over the basket and sit in the seat.

Helping a child in trouble is automatic for most of us. We do it without thinking. Since this is so obvious, you might be wondering why I am taking time to explore this analogy. I am addressing it because we want to address ourselves with our internal dialogue in a way that is similar to how we interact with children.

There is a theory in psychology that promotes the idea there are three parts within all of us. There is a parent, an adult, and a child. When we use internal dialogue, which part do you suppose is being talked to the most? The parent, the adult, or the child? With typical internal dialogue, the parent talks to the child within us. Think a moment about what this dynamic means. When we use harsh and critical internal dialogue—such as, *Yuck! I'm fat*—would we use that same tone with a child? Would we tell a six-year-old they are fat? When we call ourselves idiot, moron, and other derogatory names, would we want a child to receive such insults? If we approach our internal dialogue from the perspective of a loving parent correcting a child, we are much more likely to be positive and supportive. Just because people around us are unable to hear our internal dialogue does not mean using demeaning language is appropriate. Consider the inconsistency that most of us are kind and thoughtful to a child, but when we think about ourselves, we are often critical, discouraging, and sometimes blatantly mean to the child within us.

When I hear motivational speakers saying, "You just need to learn to love yourself," I want to gag. "Learn to love yourself" seems so cliché to me. Frequently, these speakers do not explain what it means. It becomes a mere catchphrase or a collection of buzzwords. What does it mean to love myself? Learning to love myself begins with my internal dialogue. It is up to me to develop a positive and supportive relationship with myself. Daily interactions with myself that are respectful, kind, and encouraging build a loving relationship with myself. This involves a conscious choice to use positive internal dialogue. For most of us, our lives are full of sources of negativity. The least productive thing to do is add to that negativity by beating ourselves up. There is already enough in the world that beats us up. That is why it is so important to develop a caring, loving relationship with ourselves. To support ourselves through the many challenges we encounter, it is necessary to become our own best friend.

When using the child analogy to replace negative internal dialogue, ask yourself, *Would I say this to a child?* If the answer is no, replace it with a positive statement appropriate for a child and apply it to yourself. If the answer is yes, you are learning to be constructive and supportive in the way you relate to yourself. You are being kind to your child within.

# The Five Rs

Another effective strategy to transform internal dialogue is through a process I call the Five Rs. They are:

1. **Recognize**
2. **Reflect**
3. **Rephrase**
4. **Replace**
5. **Reinforce**

This technique is not like thought-stopping or thinking about internal dialogue from the perspective of the child analogy. The Five Rs have more to do with recognizing our thought processes and deciding what we want to do with them.

## THE FIRST R: RECOGNIZE

It is important to **recognize** when we are engaging in negative internal dialogue. Sometimes it is obvious, such as when we are calling ourselves names, being critical, or putting ourselves down. At other times, the negative internal dialogue is subtle, such as when we give ourselves messages of inadequacy. We may tell ourselves something like, *I should have done better*, or *There I go again*. The moment we **recognize** we are engaging in negative internal dialogue, it is necessary to stop our thoughts and go no further.

## THE SECOND R: REFLECT

Think about the messages we give ourselves. Consciously address the negative ones. It is through **reflection** that we realize the meaning of these messages. Until we **reflect** on the messages we give ourselves, we are unable to change them. After we **reflect** on these messages, we are able to make a conscious choice not to give ourselves those messages again. For example, imagine I tell myself, *I am an idiot*. Think about this message and what it means. Do I really want to give myself this message? Do I really believe I am an idiot? When I stop to consider what the negative message is, I realize it is not an accurate statement.

## THE THIRD R: REPHRASE

Think about the messages we really want to give ourselves. **Rephrase** the messages so they are positive and supportive and address our particular circumstances. The agenda here is to not only be realistic, but to also realize we are able to be supportive and encouraging to ourselves, even when we encounter challenging situations.

## THE FOURTH R: REPLACE

Once we rephrase them, we **replace** our negative messages with rephrased, positive messages.

## THE FIFTH R: REINFORCE

**Reinforcing** the choice to use positive internal dialogue increases the probability we will use it again. If we consciously tell ourselves we have done a good job in changing our internal dialogue, the praise **reinforces** our use of positive messages so that the next time we give ourselves negative messages, we will be more likely to identify them, replace them, and not allow them. If I consciously tell myself, *Good job*, after replacing a negative internal message—*You idiot*, with, *That was unfortunate. I will pay more attention in the future*—I increase the probability I will use positive internal dialogue again because I am **reinforcing** my constructive process.

When implementing the Five Rs, it is essential to think through the process of thought replacement. It is not enough to simply stop the negative internal dialogue and throw something different into it. Just like negative internal dialogue was reinforced and developed, it is important to reinforce and develop positive internal dialogue through practice and rehearsal. The reinforcement phase helps us recognize the choices we make in not using negative internal dialogue. We are choosing to reinforce and support a positive relationship with ourselves.

The Five Rs require a higher level of awareness of the impact of our internal dialogue. Because this technique involves heightened consciousness, it offers a more thorough opportunity for significant positive change. A simpler way to think about this is that thought-stopping is two-dimensional, replacing negative with positive, while the Five Rs are multidimensional, requiring heightened awareness and conscious choices to produce lasting change. Consciously identifying and reinforcing the choices we make in our internal dialogue involves a willingness to ask, *What am I really saying to myself? What do I want to be saying to myself?*, and most importantly, *Is this the type of relationship I want with myself?* The nature of our internal dialogue is a choice. The Five Rs enable us to see it. Let us look at an example of using The Five Rs to transform our internal dialogue.

Ken has been employed at an office supply store for five years. During this time, he has worked all over the store—from the piles of paper, to office furniture, to computers and software. When a coworker struggles to answer a question from a customer, the common response is, "Let me ask, Ken." When the store is shorthanded, the manager is able to count on Ken to put in extra hours to keep customers happy. When Karen, the assistant manager, decides to quit, the store manager asks Ken to apply for her position. Ken pauses and simply says, "Let me think about it." Then he shuffles off to shelve a shipment of toner cartridges.

Ken's initial thoughts are: *I don't think I can do that. What if I screw things up? Karen's always complaining about all the things she has to do. I can barely keep track of all these toners. I don't know anything about scheduling, inventory, or ordering.*

*Do I want to have to babysit Susan, who's always goofing off, or listen to Steve's bitching all the time? I don't think I can be assistant manager. There's just too much and there's no way I could keep track of it all. I'll probably screw up, order 10,000 reams of paper, or maybe only 10 reams, and then I'll get yelled at, fired, and have to look for work. Dang, I hate looking for work. No, stay where you are, stay with what you know. Don't stick your neck out. No, don't try for assistant manager. It just won't work out.*

Let us see how Ken may use the Five Rs to transform his negative internal dialogue. First, it is important for Ken to **recognize** he is giving himself negative messages. Before he even considers the opportunities a promotion might bring, he inundates himself with reasons he will be unable to perform the job. He **recognizes** he is giving himself negative messages, such as: *It just won't work out, There's just too much and there's no way I could keep track of it all,* and *I'll probably screw up.* **Recognizing** these negative messages is not enough; it is only the first step in transforming negative internal dialogue into positive internal dialogue.

Ken **reflects** on the negative messages he is giving himself and realizes he is telling himself he is inadequate, incapable, and incompetent. He stops to think about these messages. Is this really what he wants to be telling himself? Ken realizes that through his negative internal messages, he is stopping himself, in effect limiting himself, before he has even tried. Ken considers his hopes of making a better life for himself. He **reflects** on how his internal negativity is preventing him from considering opportunities that may lead to greater life satisfaction. This reflection results in Ken understanding how his negative internal dialogue is impacting him and that he does not want to tell himself these negative messages.

After **reflecting** on his current negative messages, Ken will **rephrase** what he is telling himself. Rather than telling himself he is inadequate, incapable, and incompetent, he tells himself, *I am adequate, I am capable, and I am competent.* He reminds himself that when he first walked in the door five years ago, he did not know a felt tip pen from a ball point. Now he knows most everything in the store by its inventory number. This awareness helps him realize his ability to learn new things. By focusing on his past and current successes, Ken is able to **rephrase** his negative messages of, *There's just too much and there's no way I could keep track of it all,* and *I'll probably screw up,* to more positive messages like, *There'll be a lot to learn, but I've learned so much already since I started here. It will be challenging, but I've already proven I can learn a lot.*

As Ken focuses on his abilities, he will better realize that his manager approached him for the promotion because the manager believes he would be good for the job. Ken may also realize that since his coworkers frequently approach him or send customers to him, he is a valuable source of information and assistance. Just as he used his life experiences to validate his negative internal dialogue, by **rephrasing** his internal dialogue, he is able to transform and validate positive internal dialogue with positive life experiences.

Ken consciously **replaces** his negative messages of incompetence with positive messages of competence, ability, and capability. Although he does not know, right now, what the responsibilities are for an assistant manager, it does not mean he is incapable of learning the duties. He assures himself there will be training and help in learning his new tasks and responsibilities. If he makes a mistake, he will fix it and learn from it. He will learn the new job, just like he learned his current job.

After replacing the entrenched negative messages with rephrased positive messages, Ken **reinforces** them by acknowledging and appreciating his conscious choice to change his internal dialogue. He tells himself he is doing a good job in changing the negative internal dialogue that has been so automatic for him. He commends himself for making progress. He understands it is not an easy process, but by using positive internal dialogue he will increase his ability to achieve what he wants for himself and his life. By **reinforcing** his conscious choice to use more positive internal dialogue, it will likely become easier and easier for him to use it. With consistent practice, using positive internal dialogue will become as automatic for Ken as his former habit of using negative internal dialogue.

# Self-Reflection

Think of an instance where you use negative internal dialogue. Try out the three strategies for transforming your negative internal dialogue into positive internal dialogue. For thought-stopping, when you recognize you are using negative internal dialogue say, *Stop*, and replace that negative message with something positive and supportive, that does not deny reality. From the child analogy perspective, think about what you might say to a child and turn it onto yourself. With the Five Rs, move through Recognize, Reflect, Rephrase, Replace, and Reinforce to change your negative message.

There is no single one-size-fits-all method for creating positive internal dialogue. I encourage you to try all three strategies—thought-stopping, the child analogy, and the Five Rs—to find a way that is most effective for you. One way may feel more natural than another. You may mix and match the strategies to make the best fit for you. Be open-minded. Whatever strategy or strategies you choose, I strongly urge you to consistently practice it to offer the best opportunity for change. Remember, changing your internal dialogue requires effort and commitment to practicing, over and over, relating differently with yourself. Over time, you may surprise yourself, observing that the nature of your relationship with yourself is becoming kind, positive, and supportive.

# CHAPTER 6

---

# The Outcome of Positive Internal Dialogue

## Self-Acceptance

Take a moment to consider the expectations you may have during the process of transforming your internal dialogue. Keep in mind that even if you are committed to change, this process may take longer than you initially anticipate. If you become frustrated, think about the bumps and tumbles of learning to walk. Some days you may feel you are striding along, and other days you may feel as though you are tripping over everything and your internal dialogue is never going to change. The key is to stick with it. Remember, you have practiced your negative internal dialogue for as many years as you are old. On those difficult days, do the best you know how, get through the day, go to bed, get a good night's sleep, and start again the next morning. Over time and with consistent practice, your internal dialogue will most likely become more positive and supportive.

As you are supportive and kind to yourself and your internal dialogue becomes more positive, you may begin to feel more spontaneous, creative, and energetic. If we look at this from the child analogy perspective—where within each of us there is a parent, an adult, and a child—we may realize that perhaps a stronger integration of the three parts is occurring. Remember, in our internal dialogue, our parent within often critically addresses our child within. When our internal dialogue is positive, our parent within is kinder and more accepting to our child within. Without criticism directed toward our child within, we are more likely to experience the attributes of a child. We may feel more energetic, bright, and cheerful. We may be more willing to try new things. We may find ourselves more willing to accept new challenges. We may be more spontaneous and creative in our endeavors. We may be more playful, doing things simply for the fun of it. Our world may become less about encumbering drudgery and instead a more exciting, positive place filled with endless opportunities.

As you work to change your internal dialogue, over time the process of replacing negative thoughts will likely become easier and more natural. Some people may find the process straightforward. Others may feel stuck in their negative thinking and find it overly challenging to create positive alternatives. If you are diligent in stopping your negative internal dialogue, and continue struggling with developing positive internal dialogue, it may be beneficial to seek consultation with a mental health professional. Sometimes our negative internal dialogue becomes so ingrained there may be other factors to consider.

Seeking help is not a sign of failure or that you are not up to the task. If you seek consultation with a mental health professional to address your struggle, you will be able to share with that professional how you have tried to make changes and the difficulties you have encountered. A professional may be able to assist you in identifying variables that are intruding on your ability to develop positive internal dialogue and thus, a positive relationship with yourself.

As you become more proficient at creating positive internal dialogue, you will likely find that it is easier to see and appreciate the positives in your life. I frequently hear from people who are making progress in improving their internal dialogue that they are able to more clearly see positive aspects of themselves, recognize their strengths, and appreciate what they do well. It is as though the use of positive internal dialogue lifts a veil that had been obscuring the best of themselves from themselves. They begin believing in themselves and what they have to offer. They feel more self-confident and are more accepting of who they are. Even if they identify areas that are not strengths, they recognize their potential limitations and liabilities and are far more accepting of themselves for who they are, rather than who they expect themselves to be. Instead of being self-critical and demeaning when suffering setbacks, they are better able to objectively look at themselves and identify their strengths and weaknesses, and perhaps recognize the necessity of pursuing their goals or aspirations in a different way.

Let me provide a personal example of how I have used positive internal dialogue to enable me to overcome challenges resulting from my loss of vision. I do not wish to talk about myself to celebrate my achievements, but to illuminate how positive internal dialogue will help you overcome challenges that may be impeding your goals. When I was young, my father always impressed upon me the idea, "Don't let anybody tell you that you can't do something because you're a girl." When I was 17 years old, in two short weeks I went from seeing well and driving to being vision impaired. A year and a half later, my vision had deteriorated to legal blindness. In my internal dialogue, my father's words were transformed to, *Don't let anybody tell you that you can't do something because you're a **blind** girl.*

My vision continued to decline as I progressed through my undergraduate and graduate degrees. As my workload increased, my ability to visually tackle it decreased. It might have been easier to allow negative internal dialogue to seep in and discourage me. I required more and more assistance to cope with the multitude of information I had to digest and master. I had three full-time readers who transformed the material I was required to learn into audio format. I had publications enlarged to giant print—around font size 72—to assist me in reading along with the audio format. Classmates shared their notes with me. My exams were taken with readers. I had a guide dog to get me around campus. I had regularly scheduled meetings with professors to ensure I did not miss concepts that had been visually presented on the blackboard during a lecture. My computer was set up with assistive technology, which scanned and read printed information and allowed me to access e-mail and reports.

With all these demanding circumstances, it might have been easy to allow negative internal dialogue to exclaim, *This is just too hard. I can't keep up. Is this worth it? This is too much. This is overwhelming. I'm so tired.* Instead of allowing my daunting challenges to derail me, I purposefully used positive internal dialogue to push through the hardest of days. *Just one day at a time. Just get through today. You are able to do this. Take it one step at a time. Keep going.* I also was not above using humor to ground and cheer me up. I would say things to myself like, *Look, Cheryl, if this doesn't work out, then you've got a cute guide dog and there's always the option of selling pencils on the street corner.*

I recognized the importance of completing tasks in a way that worked for **me**. I did not do things the way everybody else did. It took me more time. It required more energy. It required more assistance from others, but it still worked for me. I listened to my strengths. I relied on my intelligence, my organizational skills, and my ability to be highly structured. I was fortunate to have a great deal of energy and drive, although I readily admit it was exhausting. To counter my fatigue, I used my internal dialogue to give myself permission to nurture myself by walking for fun with my guide dog, swimming, or taking a few moments to do something fun with my friends.

Of course, my visual challenges did not end following the defense of my doctoral dissertation. As I have matured, my visual challenges have grown more acute. My decline in vision has come in noticeable steps. Each step of decreased vision presents opportunities for renewed negative internal dialogue to seep in. I make the conscious choice to employ positive internal dialogue to overcome the increased challenges presented by my decreased vision. I may initially think, *How am I going to do this?* I then take some time to think it through, reminding and reinforcing myself of past successes. *Cheryl, you are able to do this. Remember how far you have come. Look at all you have accomplished already. You got here by thinking about the challenge and finding ways to overcome it. You have done it lots of times before. You'll be able to do it again. You will find a way. Do it your way.*

It is not always easy to keep negative internal dialogue at bay. I stumble at times, too. The mounting challenges pile up and feel overwhelming. Sometimes, I remind myself that even if everything falls apart, I may always find a can to put pencils in and sell them on the street corner. This absurdity breaks my intense negative messages and helps me redirect and focus on more positive and supportive messages. *No,* I chuckle to myself, *I won't be out there in the snow with a can of pencils. I'll be doing what I always do—forging ahead, working with what I have, and not harping on what I don't have.*

I urge you to focus on your strengths. Seek to overcome your challenges and your negative internal dialogue in a way that works for you. There is no right way or wrong way of doing this. There is no rigid recipe to follow to achieve success. Your way of stopping negativity may sound silly, like me telling myself that in the worst-case scenario I may always peddle pencils. Do whatever works for you. And whatever it is, keep doing it. Keep forging ahead. If it takes more time, then it takes more time. You may feel exhausted and overwhelmed. But in those instances, you may use the kind, loving, supportive relationship you have developed through your positive internal dialogue to get you through.

There is a big difference between positive internal dialogue, which represents the nature of our relationship with ourselves, and affirmations. Positive internal dialogue allows us to create a relationship with ourselves through conscious choices about how we relate with ourselves. Positive internal dialogue supports and encourages us. It helps us address difficult situations. It raises awareness of our strengths and helps us understand them. It assists us in recognizing our abilities and clarifies what we want for our lives. It is as though we are interacting with ourselves in a relational way. In effect, we are interacting with ourselves as we would with another person. We look to be consciously aware of the other's feelings, to interact in a respectful manner, and to be cognizant of present circumstances.

Affirmations are positive statements people repeat to themselves with the hope the affirmation becomes true for them. They are not the same as positive internal dialogue. An affirmation is more like a cheer than a deliberate attempt to understand from where one's feelings emanate. An affirmation does not take into account the relational aspect to oneself. Proclaiming yourself wonderful and happy will do little to make you better appreciate yourself if you do not identify your negative messages and recognize a desire to replace them with positive messages. Affirmations are superficial compared to transforming your internal dialogue.

Saying nice things about yourself, to yourself, with affirmations is far from harmful. Increasing positivity in your life is a valuable aspiration. However, merely saying something is so does not make it so. Affirmations do nothing to address where your negativity may be coming from. If the negativity in your life is like holes in the roof, affirmations are like buckets on the floor, catching the drips of negativity as they dribble in. They do nothing to address the holes that are allowing the drips to seep in. Not only will using positive internal dialogue help you find where the leaks are, it will assist you in repairing and strengthening your roof.

As you become more proficient at creating positive internal dialogue, you will become more aware of when you slip into negative internal dialogue. Rather than it being a normal part of your life, or just "who you are," negativity will become less frequent and thus, much easier to spot and address. Also, as you become more positive with your internal dialogue, you may find it easier to identify and address negative messages from other people. If positive, supportive, loving, and kind personal dialogue becomes the typical way you relate with yourself, you are likely to have less tolerance and patience for negative messages from other people. It is important not to allow the negativity of others to impede your progress in creating positive internal dialogue. As your positive internal dialogue evolves, you may decide to address your relationships with others who are sources of negativity in your life.

As we become more skilled at using positive internal dialogue, we may find we are more patient and positive with ourselves and other people. As we become less critical of ourselves, we may become less critical of others. As we come to recognize and appreciate the positives within ourselves, we may more readily appreciate the positives in others.

Although your relationship with yourself may become very positive and supportive, it is important to periodically evaluate the nature of your internal dialogue. Some individuals work very hard to change their relationships with themselves. Once they are successful, they stop being conscious of their internal process of creating positive internal dialogue. No matter how successful you are in transforming your internal dialogue, it is always possible to slide back into old, subtle negative messages. Remember, creating positive internal dialogue comes through a **conscious choice** to replace negative internal messages with positive ones. To ensure you are getting the most from your positive internal dialogue, it is necessary to make the conscious choice to periodically and honestly evaluate how you are doing. Yes, hopefully with practice and effort, creating positive internal dialogue will seem virtually automatic, but do not assume it will be so. Even if you are very good at establishing positive internal dialogue, be vigilant that it comes through conscious choice. Negative internal dialogue is insipid and subtle, and it may take over once again if you are not vigilant in recognizing the conscious choices you make in creating positive internal dialogue.

# Self-Reflection

Rehearsing and practicing positive internal dialogue is essential. Reflect on an instance when you used negative internal dialogue. Practice thinking how you might rephrase this negative internal dialogue to more easily use positive internal dialogue in the future. Actually consider the words you would use to create positive internal dialogue. It may be helpful to write down an example of negative internal dialogue and then practice listing positive statements to replace it. Because you have rehearsed options, you will be more readily able to use effective positive internal dialogue if similar situations arise.

Suppose I drop a glass on the floor and it shatters. I might release a string of obscenities and tell myself, *You stupid idiot! How can you be so stupid as to drop a glass?* If I rehearse using positive internal dialogue during this unfortunate circumstance, I will be more likely to use it when a similar incident occurs. If I consciously practice employing positive internal dialogue, the next time I drop something, I will be more likely to say to myself, *Whoops, I didn't mean to do that. I'll clean it up and go back to doing what I was doing.* If we have taken the time and effort to rehearse how to positively relate with ourselves, what might our reaction be when we shut our fingers in a door? We might scream in pain. But hopefully we will not release a burst of curses or exclaim, "You stupid idiot! How did you close your fingers in a door?"

We will not always be successful in changing our knee-jerk, automatic reactions to unexpected or painful events. There may be times we call ourselves names. We may angrily slam inanimate objects that, for some unexplained reason, suddenly decided to hurt us. The goal is not to be perfect, to never have strong emotions, or to never be unreasonable. The goal, instead, is to recognize the type of internal dialogue we are using and ask ourselves whether it is really helping us.

# PRINCIPLE IV

## Understanding and Recognizing Choices in Life

# CHAPTER 7

---

# Expectations of Myself and Others

To fully appreciate the power of internal dialogue, it is important to understand a particularly negative form of internal dialogue. It is powerful yet subtle, and it may be difficult to identify and change. We may use this internal dialogue without really thinking about what we are saying to ourselves. It may seem like a natural part of how we look at ourselves and the world around us, but within this language is insipid negativity. If we learn to identify this negativity and consciously change it by employing more positive and constructive statements, we will be better able to recognize choices. Recognizing our choices will lead us to feel more effective in life.

Look at these two columns:

| Column A | Column B |
| --- | --- |
| "I **should**..." | "I'm **going** to..." |
| "I **have** to..." | "I've **decided** to..." |
| "I **need** to..." | "It's my **choice** to..." |
| "I **ought** to..." | "I **want** to..." |
| "I **must**..." | |
| "I **can**..." | "I'm **able** to..." |
| "I **can't**..." | "It's **difficult** for me to..." |
| | "I'm **not able** to..." |
| | "I tried it and I **don't like** it." |
| | "It's a **struggle** for me to..." |
| | "I **don't want** to..." |

What are the similarities and differences between the two columns? Take a few moments to reflect. There are very important, yet subtle differences between them.

Column A refers to obligations and expectations placed on me from outside myself. They come from without, not within. Phrases like, "I **should**...," and, "I **have** to...," take away my choices, because they dictate what I am supposed to do rather than allow me to choose what I **want** to do. I refer to these as non-choice words and phrases or "shoulds."

Column B offers me life choices. Choices are not dictated to me from someone or somewhere else. Phrases like, "I'm **going** to...," and, "I **want** to...," are conscious choices I have determined for myself. I refer to these as "choice phrases."

"I **can't**..." takes away my power. I deny myself an opportunity before I even try. I do not attempt to explore something new that I may find rewarding. "I **can't**..." is giving up on myself. If I tell myself I **cannot** do something, it is not going to happen, because I stop myself before I even get started. If I am faced with a particularly daunting challenge and I say, "I **can't**...," it is unlikely I will be able to meet and overcome that challenge.

On the other hand, if I accept the severity of the challenge and say, "It's a **struggle** for me to...," or, "It's **difficult** for me to...," I empower myself with encouragement. Even though the challenge may be difficult, there will be options that may allow me to overcome it. If I take responsibility for my choices, then I will say, "I **don't want** to...," rather than, "I **can't**." Even if the end result is unsuccessful, or beyond my abilities, I have empowered myself through the process of transforming my internal dialogue.

# Characteristics of Non-Choice Words and Phrases

I propose that it would be best for all of us to abolish non-choice words and phrases (shoulds) from our vocabularies. This is a strong statement. However, it is important to understand we will gain a sense of empowerment when we recognize **everything in life is a choice**. There are many reasons not to use non-choice words and phrases. They take away our internal locus of control, lead us to feel inadequate, fail to take us into consideration, create guilt, and cause us to live on automatic pilot.

## NON-CHOICE WORDS AND PHRASES TAKE AWAY OUR INTERNAL LOCUS OF CONTROL

We are challenged to develop a balanced locus of control and look within ourselves to make choices and decisions for our lives. When we use non-choice words and phrases, when we tell ourselves we **ought** to do something or **need** to do something, are we really in control? Or are these urges coming from outside ourselves in the form of external expectations? Non-choice words and phrases take away our internal locus of control. When we tell ourselves, *I ought to be mowing the lawn instead of reading a book*, is the voice inside us a gentle persuasion, urging us to get outside and enjoy the smell of freshly cut grass, or a commanding voice dictating that we **should not** be allowed to relax until all our chores are done?

When we use "**ought** to" or any of the non-choice words and phrases, we are using external expectations and increasing our external locus of control. Instead, if we are saying to ourselves, *I **want** to mow the lawn because I **want** to enjoy the beautiful day*, or, *Stretching my legs and mowing the lawn will feel good after sitting here reading this book*, we are increasing our internal locus of control. Our urge to do something is coming from within. It is something we decide we **want** to do, not something that is decided for us.

We want to be careful of the words we use with ourselves. If we think in terms of non-choice words and phrases, we are automatically throwing ourselves into increasing our external locus of control. If we think in terms of choice words and phrases, we empower ourselves with an increased internal locus of control. Remember, one of the main purposes of the Four Principles is achieving a balanced locus of control.

Suppose you are reading your book and get up to get a drink. You notice the to-do list your partner has taped to the fridge. The number one to-do is, "MOW THE LAWN!" It dawns on you that the last thing your partner said before leaving was, "You really **should** mow the lawn today." If you operate according to non-choice words and phrases, you are taking away your choice of action. You are acting according to an external locus of control. Whether the shoulds come from without or within, they still lead to an external locus of control. For example, if you decide to mow the lawn because you **should**, and you know that if you do not you will never hear the end of it, you are operating from an external locus of control. If you decide you **want** to mow the lawn because it will increase domestic harmony, you enjoy a nicely trimmed lawn, and you prefer a shorter to-do list, you are operating from an internal locus of control.

## NON-CHOICE WORDS AND PHRASES LEAD US TO FEEL INADEQUATE

Non-choice words and phrases lead us to feel inadequate because they are impossible to accomplish. They direct us to focus on what we have not done, as compared to encouraging us to appreciate all we have accomplished. Suppose I tell myself, *I **should** clean my house*. This expectation compels me to go all out, dusting every nook and cranny. I move the furniture to clean underneath it. I clean out drawers, clean the curtains and draperies, wash the windows, take everything out of the fridge and wipe it down, clean the oven, and wash, wipe, and vacuum everything I am able to think of. Even the dog gets a bath. That night when I collapse into bed with chafed and pruney fingers, I realize I forgot to clean out the coat closet in the hallway. I lie staring at the ceiling, unable to sleep because I am kicking myself, *I **should** have cleaned that closet. I would have had the whole house cleaned if I had cleaned that closet. How could I be so stupid and forgetful?* Despite a long, hard day's relentless scrubbing, cleaning, and vacuuming, the should expectation is leading me to focus on the one thing I did not accomplish, instead of appreciating the huge number of tasks I did accomplish.

Non-choice words and phrases promote a subtle, but very powerful negative form of internal dialogue. We are typically not aware of how these words affect us. We use them all the time. However, we seldom stop to consider how their use injects negativity into our thought processes. Shoulds not only make us feel inadequate, they are also unattainable. No matter what we do, we will never be able to meet these expectations. Some of us may perceive their shoulds as so numerous, demanding, and daunting they decide to give up and do not try to move forward. Shoulds are likely to set us up for feeling inadequate, feeling like a failure, and feeling negatively about ourselves.

Here is an example of how the use of non-choice words and phrases contributes to subtle, yet powerful, negative internal dialogue. When some people get a test back with a grade of 98%, rather than exclaim, *Wow, what a great job I did!*, they focus on the questions they did not answer correctly. They criticize themselves, *Why did I miss those questions? I **should** have known the answers. I **should** have gotten 100%.* Rather than appreciating their successful performance on the test, they harp on themselves and focus on the questions they missed. Using the power of internal dialogue, a healthier way to approach this grade would be to commend themselves for their outstanding accomplishment and then look at the missed items.

This is not to suggest that striving for excellence is unhealthy. Rather, it is unhealthy to evaluate our worth by external measures—in this case, achieving 100%. The manner in which we strive for excellence is the key. If we are compelled by unhealthy external expectations, we are going to feel inadequate, which promotes negative internal dialogue. If we are motivated by healthy internal choices, we are more likely to recognize our accomplishments, which promotes positive internal dialogue. Getting a 70% on a test would be an excellent grade in a very challenging course if we know we performed to the best of our ability. While it may be validating to receive high grades, it is most important to gain a sense of self-worth through self-validation. In other words, it is healthier to tell ourselves—through positive internal dialogue—what we have done well, rather than rely on others to tell us what we have done "right."

A constructive way we may address perceived shortcomings is to ask ourselves what we might have been able to do differently to achieve our desired outcome. We might ask ourselves questions such as, *Did I get enough sleep the night before? Did I rush through the test? Did I read the questions carefully? Would pausing to rest my eyes have enabled me to pay more attention? Were the missed questions from the class notes or the textbook?* There is a myriad of questions we might ask ourselves to improve our striving for excellence. Evaluating potential positive changes while coming up with a plan for how to approach a challenge differently is much more effective and healthier than focusing on personal messages of inadequacy. If we function from a place of expectation, we are not likely to be successful in engaging in positive and supportive internal dialogue.

## NON-CHOICE WORDS AND PHRASES FAIL TO TAKE US INTO CONSIDERATION

If I tell myself I **should** clean the house, I am not taking into consideration whether I have had a difficult day. I may have worked long hours, I may not be feeling well, I may be tired, or I may have something else I am looking forward to doing. By saying I **should** clean the house, I am not considering my personal realities such as my energy level, my feelings, or my desires. The should is an iron-clad, no exceptions, rigid dictate that does not take into account the circumstances of the moment. Because of this, shoulds come across as oppressive and unyielding. Using choice words and phrases enables us to recognize our house would benefit from being cleaned, but will not leave us feeling inadequate and frustrated if we do not get to it the minute we tell ourselves that we **should**. If we come from a place of choice words and phrases, we will choose to clean the house at a time that best suits us and our circumstances.

## NON-CHOICE WORDS AND PHRASES CREATE GUILT

Allowing shoulds to influence our decisions may leave us feeling like we are doing something wrong if we pursue what we **want** to do. Let us look at an example of how expectations create inner turmoil when they do not match our desires.

As far back as Billy remembers, he has always loved music. He has vivid memories of turning on the radio, reveling in the magical sounds that embraced him. Initially, his parents indulged his love of music, buying him CDs, making a space in the living room for a piano, and paying for lessons. As he grew older, he became a promising musician. He dreamed of attending a premier conservatory and becoming a concert pianist. Over time, his parents urged him to spend more time on his studies than on his music. They cautioned him that to be successful, he **needed** to have a good education. He **should** go to a top college where he **ought** to study for a lucrative career, like being a lawyer or a business executive. Billy struggled and pushed himself to study. He was distracted by his desire to play the piano. He seldom got the time he **wanted** to practice, because Mom or Dad interrupted him, telling him to finish his homework. School was drudgery. Music was joy.

When it was time to go to college, Billy **wanted** to major in music, but he felt he **should not** because of the expectations his parents placed on him. He struggled with what to do. If he majored in music, what would his parents say? Would they forbid it? Would they stop paying for school? He knew what he **should** do, at least in his parents' eyes...but what about what he **wanted**? The shoulds were not taking into account what Billy truly loved to do, what he was best at, or what he was happiest doing. Because of this internal conflict, every time Billy played the piano, he felt guilty, like he **should** be doing something else. It became harder and harder to enjoy doing what mattered most to him.

Billy's conflict is he internally knows what he **wants** for his life, but he feels the pressure and guilt of not meeting the external expectations placed on him by his parents. Billy is faced with a choice. He is confronted with a dilemma of whether to abide by his parents' expectations or choose to live according to his own wishes. He is far more likely to find life satisfaction by making the choice to live the way he **wants** to live, as compared to living according to expectations placed on him.

## NON-CHOICE WORDS AND PHRASES
## CAUSE US TO LIVE ON AUTOMATIC PILOT

To live on automatic pilot means we go through our day focused on all the necessary tasks, responsibilities, and expectations we place on ourselves, without conscious awareness of our choices or what we are doing. Many of us wake up with our heads filled with, *I **have** to...I **should**...I **need** to...I **ought** to....* We go through our list of tasks for the day, dutifully checking things off. When we get to the end of the day, we may ask ourselves, *What did I do today?* Frequently, we do not recall what we did. This is because we performed our tasks without thinking about them, without being consciously aware of them, and without being present. Does this routine seem like we are making choices for what we **want** for our lives, or does it resemble the programming of a robot whose sole purpose is to unconsciously complete tasks? Imagine a little three-foot-tall robot named Cheryl who rolls around performing tasks: washing laundry, doing dishes, vacuuming, walking the dog, shopping, mowing the lawn, paying bills, and then plugging herself in at night to be fully charged, ready to go the next day. This analogy may seem ridiculous, but many of us, without realizing it, live our lives in a similar way. If we are living to complete external tasks and not making choices for our lives, we are living on automatic pilot—like a robot. Our challenge is to toggle off automatic pilot in order to recognize that **everything in life is a choice**.

## Where Do Expectations Come From?

Before we look at how to change non-choice words and phrases to choice words and phrases, it is helpful to understand where should expectations come from. When we are young, our brains are not fully developed. Our brains continue to develop well into young adulthood. Because, as children, our young brains do not have the capacity to provide internal abstract reasoning, our parents provide us with structure through should expectations. As children, when we get ready for bed, we learn we **should** brush our teeth, wash our face, put on our jammies, go potty, give a kiss goodnight, and go to sleep. When we are children, we focus on each of the tasks individually, within the should expectation of going to bed. Because our brains are effective and efficient, the should expectations involving the bedtime routine become internalized and automatic. When it is time for bed, we perform these tasks without a conscious thought. Our parents help us develop our many routines through teaching us should expectations, such as getting up in the morning, completing chores, doing homework, getting ready for bed, and so on.

During adolescence, the expectations become moralistic: I **should** not cheat, I **should** not steal, I **should** be kind, I **should** help others in need, I **should** respect my elders, I **should** respect authority, and so on. This is the time in our lives when we are developing our moral values and beliefs. The should expectations become focused on how we **should** live.

By the time we reach adulthood, we have acquired so many expectations for our lives it is impossible to fulfill all of them. We have should expectations coming at us from all directions—our work, how our home looks, and how much time we spend with our partner, children, relatives, and friends. Expectations come from our faith, our community, and the organizations we belong to. And there might be nagging expectations about not using our talents or not getting to items on our bucket lists. The list of should expectations we place on ourselves is endless.

Because it is not possible to meet all our should expectations, it would be better to stop and consider what choices we **want** to make for our lives. It would be helpful to clarify and prioritize which expectations are most important to us by changing our shoulds into wants. This step requires effort and commitment, as well as making some hard choices. We may find it is more important to spend our vacation on a trip with our children than it is to visit our elderly parents. We may find it is more important to take a job that pays less to spend more time with our family. By undertaking the challenge to remove should expectations, we gain opportunities to live our lives according to what we really **want**.

## How to Get Rid of Non-Choice Words and Phrases: Changing Expectations to Life Choices

Frequently, the should expectations we place on ourselves are things we **want** or may choose to do. It is up to us to change our internal dialogue so we eliminate our shoulds, our non-choice words and phrases, from our internal dialogue. When we use choice words and phrases, we recognize our actions are our own choices. This is much more than a matter of mere semantics—of non-choice words and phrases versus choice words and phrases. Remember, using shoulds encourages an external locus of control, where something outside of us is determining our lives, whereas using choice words and phrases encourages an internal locus of control, where we determine what we **want** for our lives.

Let us look at how to get rid of a non-choice word or phrase and turn it into choices for our lives. We often tell ourselves, *I **should** go home and clean my house.* The way to change the should expectation to a choice is to ask myself, *Is cleaning my house important to me?* If the answer is yes, I change the should into a choice phrase such as, *I'm **going** to clean the house.* If it is not important to clean the house, then get rid of this expectation and stop telling yourself that you **should** clean the house.

The next step is to adapt the choice to me. If it is important to you to clean your house, decide to clean the house in a manner that best suits you. Remember, the should expectation does not take me into account. It does not take into consideration my energy level, time constraints, whether I have made other plans, whether I have the stomach flu, or if I really **want** to undertake the hassle of cleaning when I am not in the mood. Rather than dictating I **should** start cleaning when I get home, I will choose to clean the house when it works best for me. If I am full of energy, I may choose to get right to cleaning the moment I put down my keys. If I have had a long day, I may choose to relax a bit before I start, or I may decide to only clean a little bit—like dust or vacuum—and leave the rest for when I am feeling more energetic. Or I may choose not to clean. The choice is up to me if I **want** to clean the whole house, some of it, or none of it. If I tell myself I'm **going** to clean the house, I may take myself into consideration on how I choose to do it.

Changing shoulds into choices offers us the opportunity to be creative in how we do things. Rather than approaching a task in the automatic way we have done it before, we may be creative in finding solutions for completing our choices. When considering creative options for how I **want** to clean my house in a way that best suits me, I will take into account my schedule, my priorities, my energy level, and how I **want** to be spending my time. Keeping this in mind, I may incorporate ideas like asking for help from family members or hiring someone to complete the task.

Remember, a should expectation leads us to feeling inadequate because it burdens us with oppressive and unrealistic expectations. In this case, it may be physically possible to clean the entire house after work. However, if we do so, how tired will we be? How many other things may we miss out on or not get done because we are dutifully scrubbing? A useful way to liberate ourselves from our shoulds is to ask, *Is this really what I **want** to be doing?*

Choices made with a clear appreciation of our reality—such as, *There are just not enough hours in the day*, or, *There are other* *things I **want** to spend my time doing*—allow us to feel empowered while, in this case, still enjoying a clean house.

# The Desire for Choice

Let us use our cleaning the house example in another context. If I ask a typical freshman male in a residence hall in college whether keeping his dorm room clean is a priority, he is likely to say no. If someone says to the young man, "You **should** clean your room...You **ought** to clean your room...You **need** to clean your room...You **have** to clean your room," he is unlikely to comply. A clean room is not a priority to him. However, if I am a resident hall director and I say to him, "I **want** your room to be cleaned by Friday afternoon at 4:00 p.m. If it is not, I will ask you to leave the residence hall," the likelihood of him cleaning his room is greater because now there is a choice associated with a consequence. In other words, we feel a sense of control when we recognize choices in our lives, which come from an internal locus of control.

In my discussions with parents, I encourage them to address their children's behavior in terms of choices and consequences, rather than expectations. If we say to a teenager, "You **should** clean your room, and you **have** to take out the garbage," we can expect a battle. However, if we say to a teenager, "If your room is not cleaned and your other chores are not done by 4:00 p.m. on Friday, you will not be able to go out with your friends," it is more likely the teenager will comply because it involves a choice. Most of us desire to have control in our lives. Making choices, which involves an internal locus of control, leads to a feeling of control.

Another advantage to offering choices as opposed to dictating shoulds when addressing children is that it diminishes their ability to complain that we are mean or unfair. We have already specified to them what their options are and that they will determine their consequences through their actions. Giving choices to children gives them the opportunity to behave in a manner they wish, while also learning that their choices lead to consequences. As adults, we react the same way. If we offer ourselves choices, rather than dictate expectations, we will be more successful in improving the behaviors we desire to change.

Most of us like to feel in control of our lives. If I tell you, "You **can't** have that," you may retort, "Wanna bet?" You are likely to **want** it even more because of your dislike of being told what to do and your desire to be in control. You may say something to yourself such as, *Who are you to tell me what I **can** or **can't** do? I **want** to do this, and I'm **going** to do it.* A perceived loss of control through an external locus may trigger an immediate, contrary internal locus response to reassert control and choice in our lives.

This does not only happen during interactions with others; it also frequently occurs within us. If we tell ourselves should expectations, we are likely to develop an internal conflict and protest, *Who are you to tell me what I **can** and **can't** do?* If I am dictating to others, or myself, according to expectations of **should**, **have** to, **need** to, **ought** to, **must**, **can**, and **can't**, I am likely to experience resistance. The resistance is because we desire control and choice. In situations where we feel our choices are being taken away, we may try to empower ourselves by making choices, even if they are unhealthy ones, in an attempt to feel we have some control in our lives.

One way many of us experience this sort of internal conflict is with our food choices. Think about what our initial response might be if we tell ourselves, or someone tells us, "You **shouldn't** have a piece of chocolate cake." Many of us may react to this dictate with, "Wanna bet?" This would be a natural response because we desire choice and control in our lives. We often automatically resist any perceived restrictions on our choices, no matter how well-intended they may be. When we feel control slipping away, we may feel compelled to grasp it back by resisting the outside expectation. To demonstrate our resistance, we may try to feel in control by making a choice that is not in our best interest. In this case, we might be better off not having a piece of chocolate cake, but as we gulp it down, we enjoy the perception of being in control of our lives.

Be aware of your reaction to expectations. You may already have decided to act in accordance to an expectation. In this case, you may have thought a piece of cake would be too much, and you are already full after dinner. However, when you are suddenly confronted with an external expectation that you **should not** have some cake, the initial choice of forgoing dessert is lost to the drive to express control. Your desire to be in charge has left you with an uneasy belly.

If you struggle to make healthier choices for your life, be aware of the potential for your tendency to rebel against expectations. If you react negatively to shoulds—even if they represent a healthy decision, such as not having a piece of cake when you are full—then changing the should expectation to a choice is much more likely to achieve the desired result. Rather than saying to yourself, *I **shouldn't** have a piece of cake,* it will be more effective to say, *I've decided I'm **not going** to eat a piece of cake because I **want** to be eating healthier and I'll feel better if I don't stuff myself.*

Look back on your life. Recall when you made your most questionable decisions. Most of us would say it was during our high school years. During our adolescence, we are bombarded with should expectations. The drive of many of us to rebel during our teen years is not because we are unable to recognize good choices from bad choices, but because we are straining to exercise control and choice in our lives. We often do this by automatically objecting to any directive. Our desire for choice and control is most extreme in our youth, but most of us keep this urge throughout our lives. Our scarfing down a piece of chocolate cake in response to being told we **shouldn't** is no different than the aggravating teenager refusing to take out the trash because he or she was told to do so. This drive for control is why it is so important to incorporate choice words and phrases, as opposed to shoulds, into our internal dialogue. Our tendency to automatically object and rebel against outside expectations may deflect us from healthier and more prudent actions.

When we change our should expectations into choice words and phrases, we often find our expectations are things that we really **want** to do. Shoulds are not, in and of themselves, necessarily bad. We are looking to change the should into a choice. Yes, we all **should** brush our teeth. It is difficult to argue against this, but what we strive for is to change even mundane shoulds like this one into a choice. Consciously make the choice that you are **going** to brush your teeth, rather than you **should** brush your teeth. By making the conscious choice to brush your teeth, you are supporting your desire for fresher breath, for clean teeth, and for avoiding the pain of cavities. This shifts us from an external locus of control to an internal locus of control, where we are making decisions and are not being driven by expectations.

Changing expectations to choices applies to a whole host of shoulds we may discover we **want** to be doing. Activities such as catching up with old friends, visiting relatives, saving for retirement, and many others, are often activities we tell ourselves we **should** do, but actually **want** to do. When we stop to consider these expectations and approach them as things we **want** to do, we will be much more likely to do them—and enjoy doing them. This is because we are making choices and are not being driven by expectations. We are utilizing our internal locus of control, rather than being directed by an external locus of control.

Even onerous tasks like paying bills or exercising are actually choices we make. They become easier to perform when we recognize they are tasks we **want** to do. We may feel as though we **should** pay our bills. Even though we may not **want** to part with so much of our hard-earned money, we **want**—even more—to not have our utilities suddenly cut off or our house foreclosed on. We **want** to be financially responsible, because we do **not want** to deal with the consequences if we are not. If we tell ourselves, *I **should** go to the gym,* our workout is likely to be drudgery. If we tell ourselves, *I **want** to go to the gym because I **want** to be in shape, I **want** to be strong, and I **want** to be healthy,* we are much more likely to have fun with our workout...or at least appreciate the burn.

When our should expectations involve healthy decisions, typical responsibilities, daily chores, moral values, and so on, they are much easier to perform when we approach them from the perspective of choice. We **want** to have a clean house, we **want** the peace of mind that our bills are paid, and we **want** to feel healthy and fit. By transforming these actions into choices as opposed to dictates from expectations, we avoid the inclination to make bad decisions simply to assert our control.

We may find we have a stronger sense of personal identity and awareness of ourselves as we determine the course of our lives through the choices we make, as opposed to succumbing to expectations. As we make more choices, making them becomes easier because we develop a clearer understanding of ourselves, who we are, and what we **want**.

To bring this all together, when you hear yourself using should expectations, ask yourself, *Does this fit for me?* If it does, change it to a choice phrase. If it does not fit for you, get rid of it. As you become accomplished at using choice words and phrases in your internal dialogue, you may soon realize how much more effective and efficient you are at completing tasks.

You will likely enjoy the empowerment of being in the driver's seat of your life, instead of being a robot on automatic pilot. At first glance, there does not seem to be much difference between "I **should**..." and "I **want**." Really, what is the big deal between saying, "I **should** mow the lawn," and "I **want** to mow the lawn?" The lawn is going to be mowed regardless of whether we are telling ourselves should or want.

However, hopefully by carefully reading this chapter it has become clear how making these subtle changes in our internal dialogue will shift us from an external locus of control to an internal locus of control. This shift will enable us to recognize who we are, what we **want**, and what we **do not want**. It will enable us to be more effective and efficient, empower us, and get rid of stress by removing expectations that do not fit us. Through this process, we will better overcome life's challenges and enjoy greater life satisfaction.

# Self-Reflection

Copy the non-choice words and phrases and the choice words and phrases listed at the beginning of this chapter. Put them in prominent places in your home, such as on the fridge, over the sink, by the TV remote, by your computer, or on your mirror. This list will remind you to change expectations to choices.

Changing our internal dialogue—getting rid of our shoulds—is not a part-time, emergency-use-only coping strategy. It is about changing our way of thinking all the time. It applies to major aspects of our lives—such as telling myself, *I **should** have a good career,* or, *I **should** have children*—to minor aspects of our lives—such as, *I **should** give my old college roommate a call to see what she's up to,* or, *I **should** wash the dishes.*

It applies to everything and every situation. All expectations, even minor ones, leave us with feelings of inadequacy. I encourage you to abolish **should, have** to, **need** to, **ought** to, **must, can**, and **can't** from your internal and external dialogue. Transform them into:

- I'm **going** to...
- I've **decided** to...
- It's my **choice** to...
- I **want** to...
- I'm **able** to...
- It's **difficult** for me to...
- I **struggle** with...

Using choice words and phrases like these and others, will enable you to make change in your life and ensure you are living according to the choices you **want**, instead of allowing circumstances and other people to dictate the course of your life.

If you find you are feeling guilt, it is a red flag suggesting you are operating from a should expectation. Ask yourself what this expectation is and change it into a choice. If I feel guilty I did not call a friend, I am operating from the expectation I **should** call a friend. If I feel guilty I changed my major in college from pre-med to music, I am functioning from the expectation I **should** go into medicine. If I feel guilty for going on vacation, I may be operating from expectations that I **should** be saving money and I **should** stay at work to make sure everything is done correctly. Once we have identified which should is propagating guilt, we are in a position to change that expectation into a choice.

If you grow frustrated with changing shoulds to choices, work with yourself and not against yourself in your internal dialogue. Remember, learning choice words and phrases is not something you **should** be doing, but something you **want** to be doing. As you practice changing your internal dialogue, over time it will become second nature and be easier and easier to do.

You have practiced and rehearsed non-choice words and phrases, the shoulds, for as many years as you are old. It will take significant effort to banish them from your vocabulary. Even though I have decades of practice transforming expectations to choices, I find I continually reframe and rephrase my thought processes and how I express what I **want** to say. If I find myself using non-choice words and phrases, I simply say, "I'd like to rephrase that." I then approach what I **want** to say using choice words and phrases. I recognize I am owning what I say; I am making choices and taking responsibility for what I am thinking. For me, if I let a single non-choice word, such as **should**, go by while I am talking, it is like making a crack in a dam. If I let one go by, the dam breaks and a flood of non-choice words pours out. I have learned it is better to immediately reframe my thoughts and how I **want** to say something to push them back into my reservoir of banished words to keep the dam from cracking.

I have spent a great deal of time and effort transforming my internal and external dialogue. I continue to strive to make it better. It requires consistent and conscious effort. As you begin this process, you may become frustrated and discouraged. With time and practice, it will become easier and the rewards will become more apparent. Yes, it may be challenging. Expectations are deeply ingrained in all of us, but the benefits of banishing shoulds is wondrous and liberating. In taking charge of your life, putting yourself in the driver's seat, it is vital to abolish expectations and live according to choices you make, rather than allowing outside forces to dictate what you **should** be doing.

Take time to observe and compare how differently you feel when you are operating according to choices as opposed to responding to outside expectations. Are you happier? Do you feel more engaged in life? Do you feel more in control? Do you feel less robotic and more alive? Do you feel more connected to yourself and your sense of identity? Do you feel less pressure? Do you feel less stress? Asking these questions may help you recognize the benefits of removing shoulds from your internal dialogue.

If you are feeling inadequate, guilty, or as though you are living on automatic pilot, these are all warning signs you are living according to should expectations. Stop and identify what your expectations may be. Transform the expectations you **want** to keep into choices. Discard those expectations you **do not want**.

# CHAPTER 8

## Categories of Expectations

### The Should Closet

As our lives evolve, we accumulate expectations. As we saw in the previous chapter, there is no way for us to fully meet all of them. Imagine all these expectations piled up in a single place. I call this place our "should closet." Like most any closet, there are a number of things in our should closet that no longer fit us and that we have no intention of ever using again. Our task is to determine what we **want** to keep in our should closet and change them into choices. We may then get rid of those expectations that no longer fit us or we no longer find useful.

To help us clean out our should closet, it is helpful to become aware that most expectations may be organized into three categories: developmental expectations, role expectations, and societal expectations. If we identify which category our shoulds belong to, it will be much easier to decide if they still fit and would best be changed into choices, or whether we will chuck them onto the discard pile.

## DEVELOPMENTAL EXPECTATIONS

Each one of us goes through a developmental process from childhood to old age. As we mature, we experience a gradual evolution that creates physical, emotional, and cognitive changes within us. Over time, we change and grow, and with this natural process we experience differences in our abilities. We are capable of doing different things at different points in our lives. When we are children, we do not drive cars. When we are adults, we are no longer able to fit into the tree house. When we are elderly, we are not able to run and jump as we did when we were younger. Expecting ourselves to be successful in completing all activities and tasks at every point in our lives is unreasonable, due to the natural, age-related changes within us.

Developmental expectations do not take into account the differences we experience as we mature. They may or may not fit our current level of maturity, or they may not be feasible for our current developmental stage in life.

A good example of how a developmental expectation may not fit us at one point in our lives, but does as we develop and mature, is the freshman who had little interest in cleaning his dorm room. Let us say that he is now 15 years older. He is a young professional, owns his own home, and is engaged to be married. If we ask him now whether keeping his house clean is a priority, what might he say? He might now say it is a priority for a number of reasons. He might say he worked hard to pay for his house and with pride in ownership, it is important to him to keep it clean and in good shape. He may express his desire to have a clean home to impress his fiancée. He may have simply matured and appreciates having a clean environment. For whatever reason, he is in a different developmental stage now than when he was in college.

What has changed is the importance he places on this expectation now as compared to the past. In college it was not important to him to have a clean room, so he chose not to clean it until he was threatened with being expelled from the residence hall. As an adult, with a home of his own, it has become important to him to have a clean house. In this case, the expectation did not fit him as a college student, but it does fit him as an adult. In cleaning out his should closet, this expectation—this should—does fit him. It is now up to him to change the expectation of, *I should clean the house*, to a choice of, *I want to clean the house when it works best for me.*

Let us look at an example of a developmental expectation we place on ourselves to do things that are not feasible for our current developmental stage in life. Consider a 22-year-old teacher who wishes he had the expertise of a veteran educator. The new teacher has high expectations that he will be able to easily communicate what he wants his students to learn. He immediately struggles with keeping order in his classroom. He sends more of his students to the principal's office than any other teacher. When he grades his first batch of tests and scores most of them with Cs and Ds, he realizes his students do not understand what he is trying to teach them. Meanwhile, the students of the teacher across the hall are earning As and Bs, and he never hears disruptions from that classroom.

The young teacher's expectations of his own excellence are confronted with the reality that he does not yet possess the expertise to be as good a teacher as he thinks he **should** be. He comes to realize he does not yet possess the experience and the skills the veteran teacher across the hall has achieved. His unmet expectation of immediately being an excellent teacher makes him feel inadequate. He comes to understand that earning his college degree was only the first step to becoming an effective teacher. He realizes that wishing for the wisdom of veteran teachers without having their experience is unrealistic. The expectation of immediate success does not fit him at this point in his development as a teacher, and he would be better off to remove it from his should closet. Instead, he may replace the expectation of immediate success with a desire to improve. Rather than telling himself, *I **should** be an excellent teacher*, he may replace this expectation with, *I **want** to strive to be an excellent teacher.*

Another example of developmental expectations in a should closet involves an actual closet. Imagine middle-aged people expecting to fit into the same clothes they wore while they were in college. A few of us may be able to pull off such a feat, but most find our bodies change. The expectation that we **should** be able to wear everything we once wore denies the reality that, over time, our bodies change. In this case, it would be beneficial to get rid of those items that no longer fit. It would be healthy to remove from our should closet the expectation we **should** look and dress the way we did when we were 20 years old. Instead of telling myself, *I **should** fit into these jeans I wore decades ago*, it is more constructive to recognize a choice and say to myself, *I **will** find other clothes that will make me look fabulous now.*

While many of us accept the reality we are no longer able to wear our former attire, it is harder for some to accept the reality of the changes in our bodies and minds as we mature. We may lament not being able to work and play as hard as we did when we were younger. We may curse at ourselves when we are unable to recall names and events that used to immediately spring to our minds. We may cringe at the appearance of gray hair or wrinkles. Expectations that deny the natural developmental changes of aging may produce feelings of inadequacy and incompetence. These debilitating feelings may push us to abandon activities, hobbies, and even employment that may still be feasible if they are approached in a manner that takes into account the natural developmental changes of aging. Rather than giving up tennis, it may be more realistic to play fewer sets. Rather than giving up playing with the grandkids, it may be more realistic to not allow them to climb all over you. Rather than giving up on your career, you may be able to work fewer hours. Rather than running for your cardio exercise, you may take up less jarring exercises, like cycling, walking, or swimming.

Whether it has to do with our athletic prowess, intellectual ability, or physical appearance, remember our bodies change as they mature. What we expect of ourselves may fit at one point in time, but it may not fit at another point in time. It is helpful to be fully cognizant of where we are in our lives when we examine what we are asking of ourselves. Ensuring we are in the present will assist us in determining our current developmental stage, which will help us evaluate whether what we **want** is realistic.

## ROLE EXPECTATIONS

Where did you learn how to clean your home? I learned from my mother by watching her and being under her close scrutiny as I did my chores. My mother was a stay-at-home mom until I, the youngest, was in high school. As I was growing up, I did not realize my mother was somewhat obsessive-compulsive. For her, spring cleaning was not a seasonal event, it was a weekly task. I have vivid memories of watching her each week on her hands and knees, buffing the hardwood floors. This is what I grew up with, and so I assumed this was what everyone did. Without realizing it, I acquired my mother's relentless drive for cleanliness and order, which stays with me to this day.

During my freshman year at college, my roommate was my best friend from high school. We were like peas in a pod. We were both compelled to keep our dorm room immaculate and tidy. It was certainly out of the norm from the rest of the dorm. I laugh at this now because as a psychologist I think, *This would've been a great case study.* We were so different from most of our peers. I got my first apartment the summer after my sophomore year. I loved it because I could keep it as clean as I wanted. I appreciated not worrying about the possibility of someone tracking in dirt, leaving stuff lying about, or piling dirty dishes in the sink. As I continued my studies and moved from place to place, landlords loved renting to me because their apartments were always in better shape when I left than when I moved in. One landlord, who had been leery of leasing to someone with a dog—even a guide dog—soon appreciated how I cared for my apartment. That winter, he brought me a Thanksgiving turkey and Christmas candy.

After I married, nothing changed. The house was spotless. The laundry was pressed and folded. Breakfast, lunch, and dinner were prepared and ready at their designated times. Imagine my horror at seeing my dear husband trudging across my just-scrubbed floors, his boots dripping with mud! This elicited a few words between us.

After three months of my cleaning and his dirtying, my husband came to me and said he did not know if the marriage was going to work. Not work out? How could that be possible? I was doing everything I thought I **should** do as a good wife. A good wife **should** have dinner on the table, breakfast prepared, lunch ready, a spotless house, and all the laundry done. My husband then said something that turned on a bright, glaring light bulb in my head. He said, "I didn't mean to marry my mother." In an instant, I realized I was relating to my husband in the role of "wife" rather than just being me. I was doing what I thought I **should** do as a "good wife." I realized he had not placed expectations on me. I had placed them on myself.

Our marriage was not a sudden throwing together of two people who did not know one another. My husband and I had been friends for 10 years before we got married. When he told me I was acting like his mother, I realized at the moment I said, "I do," I had taken on the role of "wife." I had expectations of what that role **should** be. I had stopped relating with him as a friend and had instead adopted the role of "good wife." After some heartfelt conversations, I agreed to shed some of my role expectations. He agreed to try to be more appreciative of how mud on my floors threw me into a heightened state of aggravation. My husband explained that he had always done his own laundry and he saw no need for me to do it for him. I said, "Have at it!" Over time, we grew to understand what set each other off and worked to communicate and find common ground—though my ground is always cleaner than his!

My role expectations had immediately brought near-fatal friction into our marriage. I constructed these expectations from what I had observed and lived with during my childhood. My husband had never asked or even intimated he wanted the house spotless, meals ready at a certain time, or his laundry done for him. He had not placed demands on me. I had placed these expectations on myself and projected them onto him. My assumptions of what I **should** be rather than who I was—and what I really **wanted**—had created unnecessary turmoil in our relationship.

What I realized would help my relationship and my sanity was to recognize that I **wanted** the house clean. It was not that my husband placed expectations on me to clean our home in my role as dutiful wife. I **wanted** meals at a certain time because I prefer a degree of order in my daily routine. As for his laundry, he could have it. Our relationship became what each of us **wanted** for ourselves and not what the other expected. Sometimes this requires diplomacy and separate arrangements. My cupboard is neat, tidy, and organized. His is crammed with all sorts of open and expired boxes of crackers, miscellaneous snacks, and 500 types of tea. My compulsion for order is, of course, a necessity for me given my loss of vision. It is necessary for me to know exactly where things are. The fact that my desire for order began before my vision started to fade is purely coincidental.

When we live according to role expectations, we deny ourselves the opportunity to live our lives the way we **want** to. If we are living according to roles, we are not being true to ourselves and who we really are. Roles placed on us, either by ourselves or others, prevent us from exploring what we **want** for our lives. Slobs who feel compelled to constantly pick up after themselves solely because it is what is expected of them will feel constantly stressed. They are living contrary to who they prefer to be. Even if our role expectations closely parallel our personalities, we will feel unfulfilled and invariably frustrated if we live strictly according to what we believe our roles **should** be.

In my case, I wanted to live in a clean, orderly home. When I pursued this with the expectation of what a "good wife" **should** be, I was unhappy and felt inadequate when things were not perfect. When I now pursue being clean and orderly, it is because it is what I **want**. I feel empowered because I am living the way I choose to live, as opposed to seeking to fulfill a role expectation of how I **should** be.

Each one of us is confronted with attempting to live up to a variety of different roles. "Good partner," "good child," "good student," "good sibling," "good person," and "good friend" are just some of the roles we place on ourselves. All these roles come laden with obligations and expectations. Every time we see ourselves being faced with an obligation, change it into a desire, want, or choice. Even seemingly innocuous shoulds leave us feeling inadequate. If I tell myself, *I **should** give Julie a call to see if she wants to have breakfast*, I may be thinking that to be a "good friend" I **should** call her to find out how her presentation went. What am I telling myself? To be a "good friend," I **should** be doing all sorts of things to demonstrate my friendship. Since there is no way to meet all the imagined expectations in the role of "good friend," I am left feeling bad about myself. This does not suggest avoiding reaching out to the people you care about. Instead, avoid doing so from the position of an obligation, of trying to meet some ill-defined expectation of how you **should** act.

Even simple shoulds make us feel inadequate. I cringe when I hear someone say, "Oh, I **should** call my friend." Even minor shoulds, ones we hear every day and use all the time, have a potent effect on how we perceive ourselves, how effective we feel in our lives, and whether we feel adequate. Instead of thinking I **should** call Julie because it is what a "good friend" **should** do, I transform my expectation into, *I am **going** to call Julie because I **want** to know what is going on in her life. I **want** to be available to support her. I **want** to meet her for breakfast because we are both early birds.* There are many choices behind my decision to give Julie a call. There is seldom just one. Choice affords us the opportunity to change an expectation into a choice. When we take the time to really think about what we **want** to be doing, we often find a ready list of reasons for **wanting** to make that choice.

Some role expectations come with conflicting feelings of obligation and duty combined with love and concern. In the role of adult caregiver of an elderly relative, we may face an avalanche of obligations that are placed on us and that we place on ourselves. Regardless of the circumstances that placed the responsibility of care on us—even if we are doing it because no one else is available—we still have choices. We are not at the complete mercy of our situation.

We may not be ecstatic about the circumstances of the choices we face in certain roles. The results of our choices might not be enjoyable. They may be onerous and downright unpleasant. It is doubtful we will ever think, *Gee, I really **want** to clean Mom's bedpan today.* We make choices that may not have pleasant consequences, but we make them anyway because they are ultimately important to us. We may choose to take on the role of caregiver for a loved one because ensuring he or she receives the best possible care is what is truly important to us. Cleaning a bedpan and other unpleasant aspects of caring for a loved one are minor components of the greater choice of **wanting** to ensure the best of care by accepting the role of caregiver.

Put simply, we are doing the things we **do not want** to do because we **want** to. The bigger choice of accepting a particular role may involve a number of unpleasant tasks, which at times may seem to deny us choice. However, they are in fact choices because they are components of the larger choice of accepting that role. Few of us **want** to change dirty diapers, but it is part of accepting the role of being a parent. Few of us **want** to wash the dishes, but it is part of accepting the role of responsible adult. Our daily commute may be a highly unpleasant ordeal, but it is a choice we make to fulfill the role of breadwinner.

When dreading an unpleasant task, it is useful to bear in mind it is merely a component of a larger choice. The tasks are not controlling you. You are directing your life. The unpleasant tasks are unavoidable aspects of fulfilling the role, or roles, you have chosen.

## SOCIETAL EXPECTATIONS

All societies place expectations on what are considered acceptable behaviors. These may be major expectations like, "Thou shalt not kill," to minor ones we may not even think about, such as holding a door open for people behind us. Expectations may involve wearing the latest fashions, driving the latest vehicles, and using the latest technology. Expectations may drive us to competitively strive for wealth. They may also involve unsafe behaviors, such as not wearing a helmet while riding a motorcycle in order to look cool. These expectations evolve from all sorts of influences: religion, culture, language, shared history, resources, climate, and so on. The topic of societal expectations encompasses a wide range of subjects. For the purpose of improving our awareness of how societal expectations may affect how we think about ourselves and judge our own self-worth, let us focus on two types of societal expectations: gender role and holiday expectations.

Gender Role Expectations. Every culture places expectations on men and women. While there has been significant effort to change gender role expectations in the United States, blatant and subtle gender role expectations continue to permeate our society. While in many professions there is equal representation of men and women, in others one gender continues to dominate. Doctors, engineers, computer programmers, and construction workers are often men, while nurses, elementary school teachers, and administrative staff are often women.

Whether we realize it or not, from a young age boys and girls are influenced by societal messages that encourage or discourage pursuit of certain interests. Boys wanting to play with dolls and girls wanting to play football are usually told their desires are not appropriate. Sometimes aspirations are squelched because there are few role models of their gender in their field of interest. An adolescent male who finds joy teaching younger children may find few male elementary school teachers to emulate. An adolescent female who is fascinated with the workings of the universe may find few female astrophysicists to emulate.

While our society looks to equalize opportunities, gender inequality with compensation and representation continues. Women may feel it is necessary to speak louder to be heard in leadership positions. They may be perceived as masculine or "bitchy" because they are assertive and confident. Men who find fulfillment in careers that are nurturing and caring may be perceived as overly sensitive, effeminate, or less than manly. When individuals violate "appropriate" societal expectations, they may experience disapproval and belittlement. They may not be accepted within the mainstream of society. This reality may encourage people with less traditional aspirations to move to certain regions of the country that are less rigid in their societal expectations.

Gender role expectations of how we dress and look significantly influence what is considered acceptable behavior. It has become acceptable for women to wear pants, while men who wear dresses may be considered outside the boundaries of society. Even Scotsmen, who are understood to be especially masculine and fierce warriors, are objects of fascination due to the unusualness of their kilts. What image springs to mind when you think of a bathroom sign? A figure with fully revealed legs is masculine—hence the men's room—while a figure with a triangular covering of the lower torso is feminine—hence the women's room. Without even thinking about it, we often define a person's gender by the clothes they wear.

Seeking a particular physical appearance is strongly influenced by gender role expectations. Men **should** be taller than women. They **should** be muscular. Women are often caught in the paradoxical expectation that they **should** be shapely, with curves in the right places, yet also skinny. While youth is prized, men are often considered "distinguished" as they age, while women are frequently labeled "old" and often struggle harder against the natural process of aging.

Take a moment to consider the images we are exposed to concerning physical beauty. We are bombarded with unrealistic images of what our bodies **should** be. Many of these images have been fabricated with software programs that digitally remove "excess" flesh from already anorexic models. Makeup covers skin variances or imperfections, and airbrushing glosses over any remaining anomalies. Striving for these unattainable images contributes to our feeling unattractive and undesirable. In an attempt to attain these unrealistic images, men and women engage in unhealthy behaviors, such as crash diets, purging after they eat, excessively exercising, taking stimulants and diuretics, and using steroids. These behaviors contribute to the development of eating disorders. While eating disorders have historically been found predominantly among females, males are increasingly afflicted with them as they attempt to meet expectations of what a "real man" **should** look like.

Cosmetic surgery, for both men and women, has become a popular way to attempt to attain an ideal of physical beauty. Procedures are given as gifts at Christmas, graduation, or birthdays. Within this generous gift is an insipid underlying message that the recipient is not attractive enough, not good enough, or is in other ways inadequate. Cosmetic surgery does not guarantee a person will meet their fantasy ideal of what they **should** look like.

Increasingly unilateral ideals concerning physical appearance deny the reality that different people have different tastes in what they find attractive. Some people prefer larger body shapes, while others prefer slender shapes. Some like muscular, while others like doughy. Some like tall, while others like short. Some could care less about outward appearances and instead focus solely on another's personality.

When trying to meet media-promoted gender role expectations, we may not consider that our partners may not find the societal ideal particularly attractive. So, while TV, movies, and magazines are filled with muscular, tall young men with high cheek bones and women with full chests and slender waists, that may not be what our partners desire. We are being convinced by gender role expectations that there is a singular ideal of beauty, while in the real world there are many different pinnacles of attractiveness. I am particularly pleased to learn some modeling agencies and toy makers are making conscious efforts to exhibit greater diversity in the images they portray. However, the majority of mainstream media promotes ideals of beauty that are exceedingly rare and unattainable for most people. There is still a long way to go before the images we receive from entertainment and advertising match the reality of our society.

Rather than pursuing unattainable, fantasy-based ideals in unhealthy ways resulting in chronic dissatisfaction, we may instead choose what we **want** based on who we actually are, our own ideals, and what is important to us. If we do this, we will be better able to find satisfaction with our self-image and more accepting of ourselves.

Gender role expectations are not solely based on appearance. Men are given expectations that they **should** not only be strong physically, but **should** also be strong emotionally. It is considered less than manly for a man to cry when he is upset, ask for help if he is struggling, or ask for directions when he is lost. Common expressions such as, "Big boys don't cry," "Don't be a sissy," "Pull yourself up by your bootstraps," and "Man up," tell males that openly expressing their emotions is wrong. If they do, they will be thought of as weak and not masculine enough.

Expectations of being strong, capable, and virile often conflict with the natural physiological changes men experience as they age. Protests of, "I can still do it," and "I've got this," are common among men who are struggling with expectations of their masculinity in the face of declining physical abilities. As their struggles become more difficult and they fail to meet their expectations of what a man **should** be, they often feel increasingly inadequate. For example, if a man expects himself to sexually perform at 65 years old as he did when he was 20 years old, this unrealistic expectation will likely create feelings of anxiety, stress, and inadequacy. The double whammy of feeling sexually inadequate and believing he **shouldn't** share his emotions makes accepting his present reality even more challenging. Frustration with being unable to accept the natural changes in his physiology and being unable to talk about what he is feeling may lead him to be unsure what to do. This uncertainty may contribute to his becoming irritable and withdrawn.

Our expectations may overlap on all three levels between developmental, role, and societal expectations. A number of simultaneous expectations are involved in the expectation that men **should** be able to sexually perform whenever the moment is right. A developmental expectation of a middle-aged man may be to expect he **should** be able to sexually perform as when he was younger. In a role expectation as a "good partner," he **should** be able to keep his spouse satisfied. A societal expectation may promote the idea that all "real men" **should** be able to perform at a moment's notice and that a "real man" **should** take advantage of any opportunity for sex.

A middle-aged woman may expect she **should** always be attractive. A developmental expectation may be that she **should** look as young as possible and avoid developing wrinkles and gray hair. In her role expectation as a "good partner," she **should** be able to retain desirability to her spouse. A societal expectation may promote the idea that aging is not desirable and may dictate she **should** look sexy and beautiful.

These examples show how we may face stress from expectations coming at us from multiple directions, in addition to the expectations we have already placed on ourselves. Regardless of where they come from, all expectations promote an external locus of control.

A healthy way to confront your expectations is to examine their source. Look to see if they are developmental, role, or societal expectations, then make the conscious choice of whether you **want** to adhere to them or not. By changing expectations to choices, you are increasing your internal locus of control. A man may realize he is physically not up for engaging sexually. It does not make him less of a man to decline an opportunity for sex. He is simply making a choice. A woman may realize she is still beautiful as she ages and there are many ways she may be attractive without trying to portray herself as younger. The key is to learn to approach life not from expectations, but from an internal locus of control where you are making choices and not simply conforming to what you perceive you **should** do or what others expect of you.

Holiday Expectations. Holidays are treasured opportunities to gather with family and friends to celebrate and commemorate the purpose of the holiday. Every holiday brings certain expectations. We often place expectations on how we **should** celebrate. This frequently turns our focus onto the chores and obligations of the holiday rather than the intended spirit of the special day. There is a wide range of holidays. In American Christian culture, Christmas is often the holiday that receives the most effort, attention, and expense. To gain a clear appreciation of the extent to which holiday expectations permeate our lives, let us look at the fictional story of Darla's Christmas.

Darla begins her Christmas planning on December 26, hoping to improve yesterday's performance. She evaluates her inventory of wrapping paper, ribbons, gift boxes, and bags so she may replenish what she **needs** at after-Christmas sales. While replenishing her stock, she usually finds some discounted decorations that will surely make next year's celebration "perfect." The new purchases are carefully stored away with all her other decorations and supplies. As winter and spring pass, she scours the internet, catalogs, magazines, and special sale flyers for just the right gift for the special people on her list. The value of each is carefully weighed to ensure everyone receives her love in equal amounts, so no one feels less loved. The purchases accumulate in her special Christmas cache. She is always careful to buy extra gifts in case someone unexpectedly provides a gift for her and she **has** to immediately reciprocate.

As the weather turns hot, the meal planning begins. *Will it be honey ham from Vermont or turkey from Georgia? Maybe duck from Delaware. Frank loves ham, but Papa loves turkey, but Steve and Emma really like duck. Turkey and duck would probably please everyone but Frank, but what about all that poultry? Maybe ham and turkey? Ham and duck? Would all three be too much? Would Connie next door let me use her oven? No, she'll have her own meal to get ready.* Darla decides on ham and turkey. *Steve and Emma will get a little extra in their stockings to make up for not getting duck.*

As the first frost hits, the details for the outdoor decorations fall into place and Frank is given his diagrams and to-do list. After years of experience, he accepts his responsibility for realizing this season's vision of the perfect winter wonderland. He **should** be able to get it all ready, so it can be turned on the moment the Thanksgiving dishes are cleared from the table. Fortunately for Frank, immediately following the Thanksgiving feast, the outside of the house, garage, and yard are appropriately illuminated, animated, and twinkling.

Now, the pressure is on for Darla. After the kitchen is cleaned and leftovers are stowed, there is just enough time to take a hurried nap before joining the Black Friday hordes. Even though she is exhausted from Thanksgiving, making sure everyone on her shopping list will get the newest and best, at the lowest price, drives her forward. After the full-contact shopping is finished, the gifts for cousins, aunts, and uncles **have** to be shipped off, regardless of how long she has to stand in line. Then it is time for the inside of the house to undergo its transformation. Pine scent wafts into every room. Santas, wreathes, figurines, imitation snow, and candles occupy every available nook, shelf, and space.

Dominating everything is the tree—a perfectly symmetrical cone of tinsel and twinkling lights with the artificial boughs bending under the strain of a lifetime of trinkets and ornaments. With the house in order and the stereo playing the season's classics, the baking begins. Cookies, pies, candy, bread, and rolls accumulate and are distributed throughout the office and the neighborhood. Evenings are filled with plays, performances, and parties, leaving only late nights for the inevitable last-minute adjustments and demands. As the long-awaited day draws near, the bottom of the tree becomes obscured by tempting mounds of brightly colored, beribboned boxes.

Darla is certain this year will definitely top them all. Everything has been mapped out and will be perfect. Everyone is going to love their gifts, and the meal is going to be delicious. Even the weather looks good—maybe just a little bit of snow to make everything merry and bright.

The cooking schedule has been rehearsed in her head over and over again. On Christmas Eve, the house and the kitchen are ready for the big day. Everything is under control. Then Darla is struck with an unexpected shock. As she stuffs the turkey Emma asks, "What time are we going to church tonight?" Darla stifles a shudder. She had totally forgotten tonight's service. Was she supposed to bring anything? Did she promise anyone she would do something? She clutches the turkey stuffing in panic. What did she forget? Was this going to ruin everything? How could she have missed something as important as Christmas Eve service? She replies with a cheery, "Ask your father," to give herself time to gather her shattered composure.

Church is accomplished without incident. No one was expecting anything but their presence. As they turn down their street, they see flashing blue lights swirling in front of their home. The driveway is blocked by a tow truck pulling a dented car from their bushes. A drunk driver careened across the yard, mowing down the reindeer and launching the inflated Frosty into the neighbor's yard. After the police have taken their photos, Emma and Steve revel in sharing their selfies with the damage, oblivious to how the swath of destruction has unbalanced the carefully constructed display or how long it will take the bushes to recover.

After a fitful sleep, it is time for stockings and presents. The box containing Emma's new cardigan is streaked with a coughed-up hairball from Bobo. Though the repulsive surprise is quickly wiped away, Steve insists on teasing Emma about her new hairball sweater. There is little time to scold Steve because the carefully choreographed performance in the kitchen is reaching its climax. Steve and Emma's banter quickly turns mean, but Frank seems oblivious to it, as usual. It takes repeated shouts at Frank to get Steve and Emma to stop bickering. At this point, Darla does not care what Frank does to keep the peace as long as there is harmony for dinner.

Instead of being greeted with bright, appreciative faces or offers to help, Darla's loved ones remain sprawled throughout the living room staring into the glow of their new electronic devices while she lugs platter after platter to the table. Frequent calls to the table fail to rouse her distracted family to take their places. After herding each individual member to the table, the blessing is given and eating commences. There are no compliments for Darla's hard work or questions of where the ham had come from. Steve and Emma can only keep laughing about how Papa's teeth fell onto his plate. Though she tries to savor the moment and the food, Darla is wracked with concern about how much Papa is fading. Then the phone rings.

Darla is irritated. Who could be calling during Christmas dinner? She lets it ring because this is hallowed family time. But she is drawn to answer it because it might be important. It is Joanne, the mother of Sarah, her old college roommate. She tearfully informs Darla that Sarah suffered a fatal heart attack yesterday evening. While Darla and her family were witnessing the destruction of five of Santa's reindeer, Sarah collapsed on her living room floor. Darla feels like she has been struck over the head with a board. Her chest tightens and the kitchen floor heaves up at her. As she leans against the counter for support, she makes a heartfelt offer to help Joanne with anything. After a tearful good-bye, Darla dashes to the bathroom. Grief and shock spur uncontrolled nausea.

Some of us may think Darla's approach to Christmas is over-the-top and ridiculous. However, I am confident most of us are able to relate to at least some part of it. Our holiday expectations may create all kinds of stress and obligations as we pursue a fantasy of perfection and harmony, which is unrealistic and unattainable. All the gifts, decorations, meal planning, shopping, scheduling of parties and get-togethers, sending out cards and packages, phone calls to distant relatives and friends, charity work, church programs, and on and on become duties to accomplish rather than expressions of love when they come from expectations. It becomes work, not celebration.

Despite expectations of love, peace, and togetherness, the realities of life continue. Loved ones fight and bicker, relationships crumble, alcoholics continue to drink, accidents happen, illness strikes, and people die. Reality is never put on hold to satisfy our wishes for a perfect holiday, no matter how much we plan or how much we desire it. It is out of our control. The problem is we feel inadequate when we are not able to meet all the expectations for the holiday we have placed on ourselves and we allow others to place on us. Because realities of life continue, we are horribly disappointed we have not attained the societal expectation of the "perfect" Christmas.

In order to assist clients in recognizing their expectations, I ask those who celebrate Christmas to identify what they **want** out of the holiday season. For some it may be to enjoy the beauty of the colors of the holiday, for others it may be to indulge in festive foods. Many seek to appreciate their loved ones and that they have a roof over their head. Some strive to celebrate their faith. Asking clients to identify what they **want** out of Christmas allows them to shift from the external locus of expectation to the internal locus of choice. When we identify what we **want,** we will likely appreciate those events more when they occur and be better able to appreciate the holiday. We will feel empowered, successful, and significantly less stressed and tired.

For me personally, I typically do not get my Christmas cards out by the "deadline" of Christmas. I do not allow myself to get caught up in the expectation that I **should** get cards out and that if I do not, I am inadequate or offending friends. Instead, sometimes I send out little notes after the holiday, maybe into the spring, that express my appreciation for their friendships. By doing this, I reach out to the people who are important to me when it works best for me, not according to a deadline imposed by an expectation.

It is important to recognize how holidays fit into our lives. For example, the Christmas after my mother died, I did not feel like celebrating as I had in the past. I chose to put up only a few of my favorite decorations. A friend gave me a tiny tree, and my family had a quiet meal together. It was a wonderful Christmas. I was still grieving the loss of my mother and a quiet, no-frills Christmas suited my somber, yet appreciative mood. Celebrating this way took me, and where I was in life, into account. If I had expected myself to celebrate as I traditionally do, I would have been miserable. I would have gone through the motions of the holiday season without Christmas being meaningful to me. Instead of attempting to meet external expectations, I focused on what was important to me at the time. As a result, I enjoyed a very special Christmas with the memory of my mother.

Holidays afford wonderful opportunities to enrich our lives. They provide us with a chance to celebrate and enjoy time with loved ones. They give us extra reasons to express love and appreciation. They allow us to commemorate and preserve treasured cultural events and traditions. Be cautious of becoming mired in the expectations of what **should** happen on the appointed day. Instead, choose what is important to you and what you **want** from a particular holiday.

Holidays may provide arbitrary expectations of how we **should** be living our lives. A great example is Valentine's Day, when people are expected to be coupled up and in love. Those who are single are often burdened with feeling left out. Many people get caught up in the expectations that if they do not have a lover, if they do not have a partner, if they do not get candy and flowers, if they do not go out to dinner, then there is something wrong with them. These feelings of inadequacy highlight the perils of having an external locus of control. These people are basing their sense of value on another person validating them.

Though I usually observe adolescents and young adults getting wrapped up in these expectations, I also see older adults—such as divorcees, widows, and widowers—struggle with being alone on Valentine's Day. I encourage clients who are single to do something for themselves that validates them, rather than feeling inadequate or seeking someone else to validate them. I suggest they have a scrumptious meal, purchase something nice for themselves like flowers, or treat themselves to something that will help them appreciate how special they are. Yes, it is nice to be validated by someone who loves and cares for us, but it is unhealthy to define ourselves by whether or not there is someone in our lives who validates us. If we are looking for validation from outside ourselves, we are putting ourselves in a vulnerable position. It is important to learn ways to self-validate through positive internal dialogue.

# Self-Reflection

The developmental, role, and societal expectations we acquire in our lives start from when we are born and continue until we die. As we mature, our shoulds accumulate and evolve. Think about all of the things we are to other people during the course of our lives: child, grandchild, sibling, friend, student, boy/girlfriend, partner, employee, spouse, breadwinner, parent, coach, mentor, respected citizen, caregiver, grandparent, and so on. At times we may feel bombarded by all our simultaneous expectations.

Regularly examining your should closet is important to see which expectations still fit you. Get rid of the ones that do not fit. Change those that still fit into wants and choices. To avoid being inundated with all the things you **have** to do and all you **have** to be, take time to closely scrutinize what you **want** and who it is you strive to be. Remember, the ability to achieve your goals is determined by the choices you make. Make choices that allow you to live your life, rather than allowing your expectations—your shoulds—to live your life for you.

To assist in abolishing your shoulds, identify several expectations that are in your should closet. Pay particular attention to developmental, role, and societal expectations to reveal where the expectations may be hidden. List all the expectations you are able to think of. Get rid of those that do not fit you. Practice changing each of the expectations you want to keep into choices. There is no single "right" way of changing an expectation into a choice. Discover ways that work best for you and that take you into account. With regular practice, it will become easier and more automatic.

# CHAPTER 9

---

# Choice Characteristics

Life is made up of choices. We are constantly making big and small choices that impact our lives. Choices range from when we go to bed and what we eat for breakfast, to whether we are going to change careers or get married. We have the choice to make healthy or unhealthy decisions. We have the choice to determine the course we take in our lives, or we may allow external expectations, other people, and circumstances to dictate how we live. It is all our choice.

Most of us do not think about what choices mean and how they impact our lives. Understanding the characteristics of choices will help us understand the dynamics involved in making our choices. I have organized these choice characteristics into the following categories:

- Choices and consequences.
- Big choices and small choices.
- Take time in making choices.

- Choices and self-empowerment.
- Choices and control.
- We always have a choice.

# Choices and Consequences

All choices have consequences. This is the case no matter how big or small the choice. It is important to consider and appreciate the impact choice consequences have on our lives. Few of us take the time to ask, *If I make this choice, what is its consequence to my life?* If we take the time to consider the consequences of our choices, we gain insight into whether we really want to make those choices. Are those consequences really what we want for our lives?

When we are very young, one of the first things we are taught is to not reach up on the stove when someone is cooking. Some of us ignored this warning once. Burned fingers instantly taught us not to do it again. "Burned once twice shy" is an obvious lesson, but many of us struggle with not appreciating the negative consequences of certain choices. A pounding hangover after a night of revelry is an obvious painful consequence, but how many people are deterred from excessive drinking by a single hangover? Decades of science has proven that smoking causes cancer and a litany of other health problems, yet many continue to puff their lives away. Some choices have distasteful consequences and others are potentially lethal. Excitement and immediate pleasure from a certain choice may blind us to its potential consequences.

Consider choices people make every day: unprotected sex with multiple partners, driving at high speeds, texting while driving, extreme sports, rodeo events, gambling, eating too much, abusing drugs, just to list a few. What are the potential consequences? For most of us, the consequences are obvious. Yet despite the risks, in the heat of the moment, we do not take the time to carefully consider what impact these choices may have on our lives. We may recognize them, but we may push them away and proceed anyway. Taking a moment to weigh the consequence of a choice could be life-changing or even life-saving. Some choices become intertwined with addiction; choosing to stop a certain behavior may not be as simple and easy as just deciding not to engage in it. However, when combating an addiction, if you are unable to make the choice to stop a behavior by yourself, you still have the choice to seek help in changing your behavior.

The most effective time to consider the consequences of a choice is before you make it. It is not effective to consider the troubles associated with being broke after gambling and losing a large bet. Recognizing the usefulness of walking is not very helpful after being stomped on by an ornery bull. Looking out through a broken windshield is a bad time to realize the dangers of texting and driving. These dramatic choices may seem obvious, but what about smaller ones? What about purchases that break our budgets? Or having coffee before bed? Or staying up past our bedtime, watching TV or playing a game? In all these cases, if someone actually takes the time to fully consider all of the potential consequences, it is more likely a different choice will be made—even with small choices. This is not to suggest choices are to be categorized as good and bad, or smart and stupid. The point is to recognize **all choices have consequences**, and it is these consequences that impact our lives. It is up to us to determine if we really want those consequences.

Determining what and how much we eat is a choice and consequence we all face on a daily basis. Our diets provide us with ample opportunities to examine how we make choices. If I tell myself I want to lose weight, then I am faced with a number of choices. The biggest is to make the conscious choice to eat differently. Everything I eat is a food choice. If I ask myself before I eat something, *Is this going to help me lose weight?* I may be more selective about what I pop into my mouth. If I know I struggle with resisting temptation, I may choose not to have my fridge and cupboards filled with tasty treats. However, if I know I have been disciplined with my food choices and there is a special occasion or an especially strong craving for a treat, I may give myself permission to stray from my diet knowing but accepting the consequence of doing so.

The choices we make are usually not an ironclad agenda, where one "bad" choice entirely derails us from what we want. We are not discussing addiction here, where one bad choice, one drink or hit, may renew a spiral of addictive behaviors. Making choices gives us consequences. The consequence of a piece of cake is not going to undo all the work of a conscientious diet plan, provided it does not induce a flurry of cake eating. Making choices is an ongoing process, and at certain times we will be more effective than others. Rather than beating ourselves up after making "bad" choices, it is more helpful to focus on the thinking that led to that choice. It is healthier to look at our choices in terms of what we want for our lives, rather than what we think we should do. We may want the piece of cake, but do we want weight loss more? If we stop to consider each choice we make each time we make it, we will be more effective in achieving what we want.

Stop a moment and think about this: Consider our options each time we face a choice. Consider the consequences of each option when making a choice. If we do this, we will be much less likely to make "bad" decisions with unwanted consequences. When making a choice, ask the following question to clarify your decision-making process: *If I make this choice, what is the consequence to my life?*

## Big Choices and Small Choices

**One big choice necessitates smaller choices.** When we make a major decision, we frequently do not consider the smaller choices that come along with it. If I decide to go to college, I may focus my attention on which college to attend given the major I want to pursue. I may weigh the pros and cons of colleges based on their cost, reputation, size, location, and climate. I may consider where my friends are going and where my parents went. These are all important variables to consider. During my decision-making process, I might not be aware of—or even think about—the number of necessary smaller choices to be made that allow my big choice to be successful.

I may not realize that to take the courses that fulfill my degree requirements, there are required prerequisites to complete that are only offered early in the morning. While this early start might not be my preference, my bigger choice of getting a degree necessitates I make the choice to get up early to go to class. Other classes in my course of study may not interest me or may intimidate me, but to complete my chosen degree, I will face the necessity of taking them despite my distaste or apprehension. Along the way, I may face other unpleasantries, such as loud roommates, nasty weather, disappointing instructors, or a general campus atmosphere that does not suit me. All these smaller variables play a role in earning my degree. How well I cope with them may be a significant factor in whether or not I attain my degree, which is my big choice. If the smaller choices become too difficult, I may question my big choice. I may choose a different major or a different school, or I may give up my studies altogether.

As a psychologist, what I enjoy the most is facilitating therapy and teaching coping strategies. If I had my druthers, I would spend almost all my professional time meeting with clients. However, there is a lot more to being a psychologist than meeting with clients. There are appointments to be scheduled, clinical reports to dictate, statements to go out, general correspondence to write, phone messages to return, and taxes to be reported and paid. There are also financial responsibilities, continuing education courses, and—my least favorite of all—insurance companies to deal with. Ugh! Coping with all these other tasks are smaller, daily choices I make that allow me to fulfill my bigger choice of being a psychologist.

All of us are confronted with big choices that bring smaller choices along with them. We might not enjoy making the smaller choices. We may, in fact, detest some of them. But the smaller choices allow the success of bigger choices. Consider some of the bigger choices in life. When I face choosing a new vehicle, I am bombarded with choices from payment options to a myriad of features and technologies. If I am serious about losing weight, I make a number of smaller choices to exercise more, eat less, and eat better. If I decide to take on remodeling my bathroom, there are a number of choices to consider from colors to fixtures. If I take a job, I face doing as my boss directs. If I choose to take a promotion at work, I may make choices to hire and fire, reprimand and reward, as well as choices to abide by and promote company policies. When I consider who I want as a lifetime partner, I am met with endless choices of which behaviors, qualities, and traits are acceptable and which will require "adjusting" to produce harmony.

If the smaller choices become too much, or too distasteful, we may decide to reexamine our big choice. We may decide the smaller choices make the big choice unattainable or undesirable. As a result, we may change or stop pursuing our big choice.

# Take Time in Making Choices

How many times have we heard, "This is a limited-time offer! Act NOW!"? A common sales ploy is to make a customer think if they do not immediately make a choice to buy something, they will miss out on a "great deal" that will never happen again. Presenting the buying opportunity within a time limit increases the intensity of our emotions. This, in turn, affects the decision-making process, as emotional intensity leads us to become more impulsive and reactive. When our emotions become involved, we are more likely to make choices out of impulsivity and reactivity, especially if our emotions are intense. It is helpful to strive to make decisions when our emotional intensity is not so high. We want to lower our emotional intensity, which will allow us to make thoughtful choices and respond without being impulsive and reactive. When making a big choice—whether it is choosing a new couch or a new partner—allowing ourselves to feel pressured because of time constraints may lead us to make decisions that have not been thoroughly thought out.

We do not want to make big decisions when heavily influenced by heightened emotions. Give yourself an opportunity to think through your decision. Allow yourself time to engage with your internal dialogue to examine the consequences of your decision. For example: *Is this couch the right color for my living room? Will it fit? Will buying it bust my budget? Was I really looking for something else?* Taking adequate time to consider options and consequences enables us to determine what we truly want.

Taking time to use our cognitive processes and think things through moderates our emotional intensity. If you feel pressured about making a decision, give yourself time. If you find yourself experiencing heightened emotions while considering a choice, back away. Sleep on your decision. Some people are able to quickly reach a decision. For others, it may take days, weeks, or even months to make their choice. I encourage you to take whatever amount of time you believe is necessary to feel comfortable with your decision. By taking this step, you know you are making a decision based on what is best for you and not outside pressures. Feeling hurried serves as a warning you may be making a hasty decision you may later regret. Give yourself permission to give yourself time.

# Choices and Self-Empowerment

We frequently face choices we would rather not make. In these instances, making a choice is, in itself, empowering. We are not always excited about every choice we make, but we make them because they are consistent with what we want for our lives. For example, considering my chores, do I want to do the laundry? Do I want to do the dishes? Do I want to clean up the doggie mess in the yard? While I am not kicking up my heels in delight at the thought of completing any of these chores, I am able to empower myself by making choices. I do want clean clothes and dishes, and I do want to avoid an unwanted squish in the yard. When completing my chores, I have many choices that enable me to feel empowered. I am not a slave to the demands of housework. If it is a bright, sunny day, I will exercise my internal locus of control by choosing to focus on the dog doo in the yard so I may enjoy the nice weather. Then I may choose to do the laundry in the evening. If it is stormy, I may choose to delay cleaning up after my beloved pooch until the weather is better and instead choose to complete indoor chores. Making these choices is, in and of itself, empowering. These examples demonstrate that even when completing mundane tasks, we have innumerable opportunities to exercise choice, which leads us to feel empowered.

In severe circumstances, we may possess few options, but we still have choices available to us. For example, if we receive a diagnosis of a severe illness, it may seem as though all choice has been removed. If we accept our physician's best recommendation as the only course of action, we may feel as though we are at the mercy of our illness and the skills of our doctor. Instead, we are likely to feel more empowered if we seek out as much information as possible about our illness, acquire other medical opinions, look at all available possibilities, and take an active role in communicating what we want with our medical professionals. Feeling empowered is more likely to give us hope that a positive outcome is possible, because we are actively involved in choosing what we think is the best course of action.

An unexpected circumstance may lead us to feel disempowered. It is possible to regain a feeling of empowerment by choosing to make something positive out of the experience. Let me give an example. Two weeks after returning from California following guide dog training, my current guide dog, Diaz, was guiding me home when an unleashed pit bull attacked him. Out of nowhere, the dog was suddenly on top of Diaz, viciously attacking him. After the pit bull was beaten off and pulled away by its owner, I tended to my stricken Diaz. When I asked the pit bull's owner for her contact information, she turned and walked away. I assumed she knew that with my lack of vision I would be unable to identify her. She most likely wanted to avoid responsibility for the behavior of her dog. After I helped poor Diaz limp home, I realized blood had saturated his fur. We took him to the vet, where his wounds were cleaned and he was given antibiotics. Thankfully, he required no stitches or surgery. While the physical wounds healed, there were emotional scars for both me and Diaz. I consulted with our guide dog orientation and mobility instructor at Guide Dogs for the Blind, who helped us work through our shared anxiety of encountering other dogs.

I readily admit I was angry and frustrated with my inability to protect Diaz and myself during this encounter. At the time, I felt helpless. I had no legal recourse against the pit bull's owner because I did not know who she was. Instead of allowing my feelings of being victimized to interfere with my life, I chose to make something positive out of this horrible experience. I resolved to take action to reduce the likelihood this would happen to us again—or to anyone else. This attitude blossomed into my writing a professional article with Marc Gillard, our guide dog orientation and mobility instructor. The article, "Assisting Handlers Following Attacks on Dog Guides: Implications for Dog Guide Teams," presents a protocol for dog guide orientation and mobility instructors to assist guide dog teams and for handlers to assist themselves in coping with trauma following a dog attack.

I have presented this paper at conferences in the U.S., France, and New Zealand. I worked with a local newspaper and a TV news station to generate awareness of leash laws and laws protecting service animals. It was only after these stories came out that a man who lived in the area of the attack approached me to tell me he had seen this woman before with her dog off leash and that it was a pit bull. While the experience of the attack on Diaz remains raw to me, I have transformed it into a passion for protecting guide dog teams from these all too frequent, senseless, and preventable attacks. I continue to be a staunch advocate for the protection of guide dog teams. My ongoing efforts provide me with a positive outlet for my heartfelt emotions. It enables me to feel as though I have some impact in reducing the chance my Diaz and I will endure something like this again. Unfortunately, recent attacks on other guide dog teams have shown there is still much work to do in raising awareness about this issue.

Even seemingly debilitating experiences that come from nowhere present us with opportunities to make choices that promote feelings of empowerment. We are not helpless to the whims of fortune. Taking negative experiences and choosing to transform them into positive actions provides us with a healthy avenue for empowerment. Our experiences do not have to dictate the course of our lives. We may all empower ourselves to make choices that chart our own course toward what we want, even when we face challenging circumstances.

# Choices and Control

As stated earlier, there are many times in life when we face choices we really do not want to make. We desire to feel in control of the choices available to us. However, some circumstances are immune to our efforts to change them. They are given to us, whether we like it or not. When we are confronted with an unwanted circumstance, a productive way of addressing it is to determine whether it is changeable. For example, an inoperable tumor may not be changed. A spouse seeking a divorce may be changeable depending on the nature of the relationship. A layoff notification may be unchangeable. Underperforming investments are changeable. Some situations are more in our control than others. Some are completely out of our control.

Repeatedly trying to alter an unchangeable circumstance is futile and ineffective. Attempting it is like hitting our heads against a brick wall. The wall is not going to change under the impact of our heads, but we will certainly suffer a great deal of pain. Rather than suffering needless pain and wasting effort and emotional energy trying to change the unchangeable, it is better to recognize the reality of what is given in life. We are only able to be effective after we accept the reality of our given circumstance. Then we may consider the available choices.

While few of us would be foolish enough to try to head-butt our way through a wall, unexpected challenges are seldom as obvious and easy to spot as bricks. If you are having difficulty overcoming an unexpected challenge, carefully evaluate whether you are trying to pound your way through an unyielding brick wall. If you are, step back and identify how you may approach the challenge in a more productive and effective way by not attempting to change the event, but by working within the constraints of the reality.

Consider the challenges of a family member suffering with an addiction. You may attempt to combat their addiction in a number of ways. You may think monitoring their addiction and keeping them informed about how much they are consuming will make them aware they are consuming too much. You may make excuses for their failure to meet their responsibilities. You may dismiss that there is a problem and say their behaviors are just "who they are." You may try to cure their addiction with love or provide them money and other assistance to alleviate the stressors supposedly contributing to their addiction. Even though these efforts may show no sign of stopping the addiction, you may repeatedly try them in the hope that something—anything—will make them stop. It does not stop. This case is an instance of hitting your head against a brick wall.

If your attempts to combat a loved one's addiction have not been effective, the only way to be productive is to accept the reality that the situation is out of your control. It is not within your control to manage the behavior of someone else. The loved one will only be able to address their addiction when they choose to do so. Your choices will not affect the reality of their addiction. If they choose to get help, you may choose to support them. If they choose not to address their addiction, your choice may be to stop monitoring their consumption, stop making excuses, and essentially stop enabling them by shielding them from their responsibilities. You will be making choices for your own life, rather than allowing the choices of others to control you. If you find it difficult to let go of the choices of others, you may find encouragement by engaging in support groups and therapy.

Our given circumstances are like cards dealt to us. It is up to us to recognize we have been dealt a card, pick it up, and see what it is so we may play it in the most effective way possible. When confronted with an unexpected circumstance, many people ask themselves, *Why did this happen to me?* This question only serves to make the situation more stressful and difficult. Asking why is a futile cognitive exercise. I may ask 50 people why something occurred and receive 50 valid answers. The multitude of potential valid answers overwhelms us and leaves us feeling like a top spinning in place, going nowhere. To be effective, the question to pose is not, *Why?*, but, *Given this situation, what may I do now to address the circumstance?*

A child stricken with cancer is a horrifying circumstance. A common response is to ask why because it is so contrary to our innate sense of fairness. Asking for a reason for this sort of tragedy only serves to deflect us from more effective ways of coping. Asking why is often a knee-jerk reaction to any bad experience. Many of us ask, *Why me?*, after a car wreck, our partner cheats on us, our investments plummet, our house burns down, or we are mauled by an escaped zoo animal. If we are able to understand a reason behind our given circumstance, we may think we have control of the situation when, in fact, we have none. Thinking a misfortune is a reaction to some misdeed and that correcting our behavior will correct the misfortune is an attempt to seek control when, in reality, there will never be a good enough explanation as to why certain events occur.

Seeking control is a natural response. Some circumstances are beyond our control. To cope effectively, it is crucial to recognize the reality of what is given in your life. You are only able to be effective once you accept the reality the given circumstance is not changeable. Then, by working within the constraints of your reality, consider the choices available to you and make choices that lead you to feel more in control.

## We Always Have a Choice

Thinking I do not have choices is not accurate and limits my options. At some points in our lives, we may confront unexpected events and challenges that appear to deny us choices. Despite the severity of an event, there will always be a circle of choices to make. Suppose you receive a terminal diagnosis and you have only a few months to live. With no curative options available, it may seem as though all opportunities for choice have been taken away. However, even with only a few months left to live, there are a number of choices you are still able to make. How do you want to spend the days you do have? Are there things you want to accomplish before you die? Where do you want to die? Who will you inform about your condition? Who do you want with you in your final days? Who do you want to talk with before you die? Is there something you want to say? Who do you want to get your belongings? Even in the most difficult times, when we are given circumstances we prefer not to experience, there are still opportunities to make choices.

Let me share my personal story of when I was abruptly confronted with vision loss and it seemed like all my life plans were no longer an option. Before I began to lose my vision, I had my life mapped out. I was going to choose a pre-med major in chemistry, with a minor in piano performance. I hoped to go on to medical school to become a pediatrician. With my sudden loss of vision, my aspirations for the future evaporated. It seemed like all my choices had been snatched away. There was no hope of achieving my goals, so what was I to do? It would be dangerous for me to work closely with chemicals if I could not see what I was doing.

While being unable to pursue my career choice was intensely disappointing, I resolved to determine what choices I had available given the reality of my limited vision. I still wanted to go to college. It was up to me to find a new preferred course of study. Yes, the number of choices had dwindled considerably, but I still had many choices available to me. Music therapy combined my love of music and my interest in healing. It became my undergraduate major which, through a series of choices over time, led me to psychology.

Once we recognize and accept the reality of a situation where our choices have been severely curtailed, we will find we still retain a number of choices. The initial shock of an unexpected circumstance may temporarily blind us to our options, but if we examine our situation, we will realize we still have opportunities to make choices. We may find that as we begin to make choices within the limitations of our new reality, new opportunities open up to us. In my case, music therapy opened up into a busy psychological practice and being actively involved in organizations that advocate for people with disabilities.

Take a moment to carefully consider the following: If I perceive I have no choices, I am limiting myself. Even in extreme circumstances, there will still be choices available. If you feel like nothing is left for you to decide, carefully examine your circumstances. It may require a shift in your thinking to accept the reality of your current circumstances. Ask yourself this question: *Given my situation, what choices are available to me now?* Even though we may not be thrilled with the choices we face, there are always choices available to us.

# Self-Reflection

For some people, recognizing that **everything in life is a choice** is a very scary idea. Realizing the choices we make directly impact our lives may be overwhelming and frightening. Some people avoid making choices because they do not want the responsibility for making them. It is easier for them to allow events and opportunities to pass them by, rather than actively engage in life. However, making the choice to not make choices is, in itself, a choice.

We are shaped by the choices we make. Do not allow decisions that turn out badly to deter you from making future choices. We often learn more about ourselves from our mistakes than from our successes. Allowing others to make choices for us, when we abdicate making decisions, denies us opportunities to learn what we truly think, feel, and desire. Making choices gives us the power to create what we want for our lives. How would you know if you like Chinese food if you never made the choice to try it? How would you know if you feel better living in the country if you never made the choice to spend time in cities? How would you know you have artistic talent if you choose never to pick up a paintbrush or a musical instrument? If I had not made the choice to try to write this book, what would you be reading right now? Making choices clarifies how we desire to live life.

Think about the different characteristics of choices presented in this chapter. Think about the choices you have made in your life that represent these characteristics. Reflect on how they altered your life. What were the consequences? Did your big choices produce a number of smaller choices you had not considered? Did you have time to carefully think things through, or were you in a heightened emotional state? Was making choices empowering for your life? Did you gain control of the situation? Were you able to identify that you had choices?

Reflect on choices you have made and how you made them. They may reveal a pattern in how you make choices. If you are unhappy with the results of your choices, you may be better served by changing the pattern of how you make choices. Employ the concepts behind choice characteristics to alter your approach to making choices. Consider the consequences of your choice before you make it. Consider little choices that may come with a big choice. Make sure you give yourself enough time to consider your options in making choices. Remember, even though a choice may be difficult to make, making it will lead to feeling empowered. As you make more effective choices, you will likely feel more in control of your life. Most importantly of all, remember that we always have a choice.

# CONCLUSION

---

# The Four Principles and Life Satisfaction

# CHAPTER 10

---

# Tying It All Together

$E$very day, we all face challenges that impede our ability to find life satisfaction. Some challenges may be relatively mundane, such as balancing chores with having time to relax. Some challenges may be a constant, chronic irritant, such as an unfulfilling job or an unhappy relationship. Some challenges may be totally unexpected, such as our car getting totaled in a parking lot. Some challenges are slow but inevitable, such as figuring out what we are going to do when we retire. With all the challenges we face—from the small to the earth-shattering, from the unexpected to the inevitable—we will find greater satisfaction in our lives if we employ the Four Principles. Again, the Four Principles are:

Principle I: Self-nurturing and taking care of myself

Principle II: Learning to live in the present

Principle III: Developing a positive relationship with myself

Principle IV: Understanding and recognizing choices in life

Regardless of the challenges we face, it is vital to make the conscious effort to nurture ourselves so we have strength and energy to cope. By eating well, getting rest, exercising, engaging in activities for fun, and appreciating the small, beautiful things in life, we will ensure our water pitchers—our reservoirs for coping—are as full as possible. Each water pitcher is different. Some of us may cope more easily with challenges than others. Taking the time to self-nurture will ensure our water pitcher is as full as possible so we are at our best when we face a challenge.

The only place we are able to effectively face life's challenges is in the present—this moment, this second. We are unable to change our past, and the future has not yet arrived. Living in the past promotes depression and living in the future creates anxiety. By staying in the present, we are able to actively make change in our lives.

It is not as likely we will be successful in overcoming our challenges if we are critical, demeaning, and doubtful of ourselves and our abilities. By consciously developing a positive relationship with ourselves in a manner that does not deny reality, we will be better able to identify and employ our strengths. We will avoid negativity that may deflect or discourage us.

Everything in life is a choice. Despite the severity of the challenges we may face, there will always be choices available to us. By recognizing these choices and selecting the ones that best suit us, we will gain feelings of control and empowerment. If we approach our challenges by the choices we make, rather than by expectations we place on ourselves and others place on us, we will live our lives as fully as possible.

Up to this point, the Four Principles and their components have been presented individually, along with examples, to show how they work and how to develop each skill. There are often a number of factors influencing our decisions, and some factors weigh more heavily than others. The Four Principles are used in concert with each other to provide us with the best possible means of overcoming our challenges. Each principle builds upon the other, and as we become more familiar with them, we will find we are using them simultaneously. This takes time and practice, but with conscious and consistent effort, we will experience improvement in how we cope with life's challenges and enjoy greater life satisfaction.

The Four Principles apply to most challenges, no matter how big or small, or whether they are expected or unexpected. To show how the Four Principles work together to improve life satisfaction, let us look at a few examples. While some of the following examples may seem extreme, the reality is it is not uncommon for us to face extreme challenges in our lives. These examples are presented to show how the Four Principles work well for most anyone, whether young or old, healthy or sick, destitute or wealthy. They are intended to assist us in seeing how we may use the Four Principles in our own lives.

These stories are completely fictional scenarios that demonstrate how the Four Principles may be applied in a wide range of circumstances. The first story is a brief vignette, then each subsequent story builds in complexity. The later examples are more descriptive and do not explicitly identify how the Four Principles are used. In these examples, you are encouraged to identify ways the characters are implementing the Four Principles. This exercise is intended to assist you in applying them in your own life.

# Sand in the Hourglass

Sandy never has enough time. Work takes at least 50 hours a week. She strives to take care of the needs of her elderly mother, two teenage sons, and husband—all of whom are always wanting her to do something for them. She is the one in charge of managing the house, completing housekeeping chores, getting the shopping done, and cooking. She is a fixer, smoothing out family arguments and soothing disappointments. She is always trying to keep everyone happy. Sandy always feels stressed. There are almost no moments in the day when she is able to relax. How may Sandy apply the Four Principles to address the stress in her life?

It will be helpful for Sandy to take time for herself, to know it is not necessary to always be available to everyone at all times. It will be helpful for her to recognize it is acceptable to say no to people. Sandy may be telling herself she is inadequate and ineffective when she is unable to meet other people's expectations. She will benefit from changing her internal dialogue from being punitive when she is unable to comply with a request, to being positive and supportive of herself. Unrealistic should expectations lead her to experience negative internal dialogue. It would be best for her to change her should expectations to choices like, *It is unrealistic for me to be available to everyone at all times. I will do the best I am able.* In this way, she will be able to say she is doing a good job, is accomplishing tasks, and is effective. Instead of telling herself, *I am a failure*, for not completing one specific task, she will use positive internal dialogue and tell herself, *I got a lot done today*.

It is important for Sandy to make and protect time for self-nurturing. Rather than bulldozing through her day, she will greatly benefit from setting aside time to exercise, engage in hobbies, and stop long enough to appreciate the little things around her. By making the conscious effort to set aside time just for her, she will fill her water pitcher and have a greater reservoir for coping with and meeting the challenges in her day. Sandy may tell herself she does not have time to self-nurture. However, she will find if she takes time for herself in the short run, she will have more water in her pitcher for coping in the long run.

Sandy constantly focuses on what to do next. Her persistent future orientation causes her to feel stressed and anxious. She will feel more effective and efficient if she stays present and approaches tasks one at a time. Sandy will benefit from giving herself permission to accept she might not accomplish all the tasks as quickly as she would like. She may choose to prioritize which tasks are most important to complete, recognizing and accepting that all the tasks might not be completed in one day or at one time. If there is a special occasion to prepare for, Sandy might ask herself, *What may I do today to make my tomorrow what I want it to be?* This question may help her determine what is most important to address now.

Sandy will benefit from increasing her internal locus of control. She will feel more empowered as she recognizes she has choices with everything she does—including when, how, and if she does something. It will be beneficial for her sons to learn greater responsibility in taking care of themselves, rather than relying on Sandy for everything. Sandy will benefit from examining role expectations of what she believes is important in her roles as a daughter, mother, and spouse. Declining a request in any of these roles does not automatically mean she is a bad daughter, mother, or spouse. Instead, she is prioritizing what is important for her and her life at that moment. As she increases her internal locus of control, she will feel better able to manage her life, rather than her life dictating all the things she should do.

# Dear John

John is a lover. He is always on the lookout for a new sexual partner. He thrives on the interest strangers show him. The attentiveness in the eyes of a stranger makes him feel desirable, important, and worthy. Each new partner is a testament to his virility and attractiveness. After every encounter, John never feels as good as he hoped he would. The thrill of the moment fades, and he is left feeling empty and alone. Though he feels aching loneliness, his first thought is to discard his latest lover with as little fuss as possible.

John tells himself that more than anything he wants to find someone to share his life with, someone to talk to about anything and do fun things with. He tells himself he wants to stop pretending to be someone else to lure a new lover into his bedroom. He tells himself he wants a lasting, loving relationship, but he never seems to be able to find that "right" person. Some lovers show promise, like they might be the one, but they inevitably do something that turns him off, or he becomes bored and they end up being just another notch on his bedpost. Despite John's expressed intention of wanting to develop a meaningful relationship, he continues to engage in casual sexual encounters. How may John apply the Four Principles to develop meaningful relationships in his life?

John shows little concern for his own health by roving and being indiscriminate with sexual partners. This behavior may make him vulnerable to diseases that may result in severe consequences for his health and his life. Since sexual gratification only provides fleeting pleasure and ultimately leads John to feeling unfulfilled, he will benefit from gaining lasting satisfaction in ways that do not involve sex. He may find hobbies, sports, and activities provide him with more pronounced feelings of enjoyment and more readily fill his water pitcher.

It will be advantageous for John to consider what he wants to invest in today toward what he wants for tomorrow. If a long-term relationship is what he truly wants for his future, his current practice of short-term gratification will not build a foundation for a significant long-term partnership. His focus on immediate, short-term pleasure makes him unavailable to opportunities for establishing a potential lasting relationship. The energy he currently gives to his partners is solely to get them into bed.

John faces the challenge of looking at himself and deciding what he wants for his life. His locus of control is almost exclusively external. He gains validation from other people who think he is desirable. John will greatly benefit from looking within himself to build a stronger internal locus of control. Before he is able to have a meaningful relationship with someone else, it is necessary for John to first build a nurturing relationship with himself. He will benefit from discovering who he is, other than a lover. Up to this point, John has defined himself mostly in terms of his ability to get other people into bed. This single dimension is not enough to sustain the substantial relationship he expresses he desires.

John will be aided in his search for a committed partner if he examines his own qualities. He may ask himself searching questions to discover who he is, such as: *What am I good at? What activities do I enjoy besides sex? What are my beliefs and values? How am I able to feel good about myself in ways other than being sexually attractive?* By examining other aspects of his personality, John may discover he has many other attributes besides sexual attractiveness. He may come to appreciate he has more to offer a relationship than just sex. Because of this realization, John will be more likely to develop deeper, more lasting bonds with another person.

John might discover unrealistic expectations are preventing him from developing a significant relationship. John's perception that his manliness is dependent upon making as many sexual conquests as possible will impede his ability to be more selective in choosing a partner. If he perceives a gender role expectation that men should have as many partners as they are able, he will find it difficult to establish a sense of specialness with anyone. His gender role expectation that he should never decline sex may interfere with his ability to be monogamous, and monogamy will likely be a cornerstone of any significant relationship he tries to develop.

John's expectation that there is such a thing as a perfect partner is unrealistic. His habit of terminating a relationship the moment his partner says or does something he finds unattractive or boring prevents John from engaging in a realistic relationship. Everyone has flaws and quirks. No one is perfect. A meaningful relationship involves appreciating a person for who he or she is. John will benefit from asking himself what he wants from a committed partner: *What traits in another person are important to me? What are their interests and activities? What are their beliefs and values?* By asking himself these questions, what he truly wants in a partnership may become clearer to John. By determining what he wants in a partner, John may become more willing and able to accept minor unappealing quirks, instead of instantly dismissing a lover the moment he discovers them.

John may use his internal dialogue to stop relating to the world around him in strictly sexual terms. Instead of telling himself, *I need to hook up with someone soon,* he may say, *I'm going to see about joining a softball league,* or, *I'm going to sign up for the office 5k charity walk and go to the barbecue afterward.* After relating with himself in a more positive manner, his internal dialogue may change from, *I'm the man for hooking up three times this week,* to, *I'm the man for driving home the winning run,* or, *I'm the man for raising a lot of money for the office charity.*

As John realizes, through his internal dialogue, that he has much more to offer besides sex, he may be better able to appreciate that people also have other qualities and more value than sexual appeal. He will do well to replace the internal messages that evaluate people strictly on the basis of their sexual attractiveness. Instead of saying to himself, *That person is hot,* he may say something like, *That person has a nice laugh,* or, *That person said something quite interesting,* or, *I laugh at that person's jokes.*

It will be beneficial for John to stay present, rather than focusing on his next sexual encounter. If he finds himself fantasizing about who his next lover may be, he may say to himself, *Stop. What do I want to do right now?* This action will help break his pattern of thinking about his next lover. The objective is to stay present with whatever he is doing, wherever he is—whether that is at work, preparing a meal, or taking a walk in a park. This strategy will help him remain in the present and appreciate life now.

# Leaving the Nest

Steve likes staying up all night playing video games while most of the "morons" are asleep. He hates his teachers and his classmates. He hates getting up in the morning. He hates getting "nagged" about his homework. Most of all, he hates it when anyone tells him what to do. He does just enough work to make sure he passes his classes. In just a few months, he will graduate and no one will be able to tell him what to do.

Steve's mom is on him all the time about his plans after graduation. If he is not going to go to college or learn "some stupid trade," like becoming a plumber or an electrician, then he needs to get a job. But at whatever "stupid job" he gets, there will be some "stupid idiot" telling him what he should be doing. There is the military, but that would be the worst of all, with people yelling at you 24/7 and living with a bunch of "gung-ho jerks." Mom threatens that if Steve is not working full time within a month of graduation, she will boot him out and he can live with his "worthless father." But there is no room for Steve at Dad's, in his tiny shack-of-a-house with his "bitchy" stepmom and their brood of four "whiny pests" (two from Dad, and two from some other guy before she latched onto him).

Steve just needs time to think about things without being hassled. He needs some time in the basement playing video games, watching videos, and surfing the net. He will get it all worked out. It will happen. After all the work at school, he deserves some time off.

The blessed graduation day finally comes and goes. Things are good for a few weeks, except for Mom's constant harping on Steve to get a job. He leaves a few applications lying around to make her think he is looking for work. He hopes it will get her off his back, but nothing seems to shut her up. Every day he hears, "Who have you interviewed with? What are you going to do? I'm not going to keep paying for you to sit on your ass all day!" On and on and on.

After six weeks of her constant badgering, Steve's mother cuts off the internet service. He is so angry he knocks down her "stupid" knickknack shelf. Mom hides his car keys because she took Steve off her insurance. Steve can't take it anymore and leaves to crash on a friend's couch. A few days later, he comes home to find all his belongings heaped in a corner of the garage. Steve confronts Mom. She bluntly tells him he is no longer welcome at the house. If he isn't going to help out and pay his own way, he can mooch somewhere else. She is done. No amount of screaming at Mom changes her mind. Mom has "turned her back" on her only son. Why live with a "monster" like that?

Steve goes back to his friend's couch for a few days. His friend's folks soon kick him out because they "want their house back." A few other friends put him up here and there, but it is soon the same story, the same "nagging," the same wanting something from him. After pawning most of his belongings and moving from place to place for a few months, Steve's friends stop returning his texts. The only place he is able to crash is a small-time drug dealer's "crappy apartment that reeks of cat piss." Steve does not trust the dealer. The dealer is unpredictable, and his friends are sketchy. Steve fears he will end up in jail from trouble they might get into. That would be worse than living with Mom. Steve starts asking himself, *How did things get so bad? How am I going to be able to have my own place, with my own stuff, that no one else can take away from me? What now?*

How may Steve apply the Four Principles to build the life he wants? Steve faces a crucial choice. He is at a crossroads in his life. He may continue looking outside himself to other people for food and shelter (external locus of control) or he may decide to look within himself to find ways to provide his own food and shelter (internal locus of control). What are his options? He may choose to continue doing what he has been doing, which may result in substance abuse, crime, jail, and physical danger, or he may come up with a plan of action that allows him to build a life in which he makes more effective decisions. He does not want to be like the dealer's sketchy friends. He knows he is better than that, but the other choice (building a life) seems so hard. He perceives everyone has abandoned him, including his mother.

After understanding choices and consequences, Steve comes to realize the path he is on will lead to nothing but trouble—and maybe an early grave. The best way to get the life he wants is to change his choices. To do this, he realizes it may be necessary to do some "crappy jobs" and be nice to some "crappy people," but these will be steps toward where he wants to go. It would be productive for Steve to alter his thought process from, *I need to get some crappy job to get money,* to *I'm going to get a job to earn the money that will allow me to build the life I want for myself.* Steve replaces the should expectation of needing to get a job with a choice of going to get a job.

Steve may take whatever job he is able to find to earn some money. He may contact an employment agency to find out if there are job training programs available. He may go to various charity groups to acquire appropriate work clothes and food. He may live in a shelter for a time to avoid the dangers of living with the dealer. He may seek to reconnect with his mother by demonstrating he is serious about getting his life on track. As he starts working and taking care of his immediate demands for food and shelter, he may explore the possibilities of vocational training or community college to gain marketable skills. As Steve makes one constructive choice after another, more opportunities are likely to open up to him. Steve continually faces the choice of whether to make constructive or destructive choices. The opportunity to make destructive choices is always present. Every day is full of choices.

Self-nurturing will allow Steve to more easily make constructive choices and resist making destructive choices. If Steve eats healthfully, has a consistent sleep schedule, and exercises, he is likely to find work less of an ordeal. To get enough restful sleep, he will find he is better off setting limits on the amount of time he plays video games. He may learn that when he does his own cooking, rather than eating fast food, he feels better and saves money.

By trying out new activities, he may discover new interests and meet new people. He may enjoy bowling, playing pool, and working out. He may decide to learn to play the guitar or some other musical instrument. He may consider learning computer programming to create his own video games. Steve may benefit from taking time to appreciate pleasant aspects of the environment around him. For example, he may take a few moments to watch squirrels bounding from tree to tree, gaze at an interesting sky, or listen to street musicians. He may occasionally spend a bit of extra money to have an especially good meal or buy a new game to reward himself for the progress he is making. All these are examples of self-nurturing at the primal, play-recreational, and naturally occurring phenomena levels.

Steve has difficulty living in the present. His impatience for wanting a life where he is able to do what he wants to do, when he wants to do it, interferes with his ability to follow through with the tasks necessary for obtaining the money and skills to live independently. By daydreaming about how great the future will be once he has everything he wants, he misses out on taking necessary steps to make his future dream a reality. It will benefit him to realize that while he feels like staying in bed and skipping work, it is more productive for him to go to work today so he has enough money for food and rent tomorrow. Each day of work is a step toward his financial independence. His work today is the only way he will be able to achieve the life he wants in his future. He may identify goals for his life that direct his behavior today. Instead of wasting time fantasizing about his dream home, dream car, and dream girl, and lamenting about what he does not have, it will be most helpful for Steve to ask himself, *What do I want to invest in today that will make my tomorrow what I want it to be?*

Given Steve's habit of blaming others, he is especially challenged to take responsibility for his choices and live in the present. By ruminating on the perception that his situation is due to perceived wrongs he has suffered in the past, he may struggle to take positive action. Instead of blaming his mother for his living options being reduced to sleeping in a shelter, it will be best for Steve to recognize the importance of developing an internal locus of control and consider what he may do today to make his life better. The evolution of his life is not about his mother or what she has "done to him." Mom is no longer impacting his life. Steve's life is about Steve and the choices he makes today to make his life better. Rather than ruminating about the past, it will be constructive for Steve to ask himself, *What have I learned from this that I am able to use today?* It is important for Steve not to dwell on his past, because it drags him down and prevents him from making choices that will improve his present. Steve may instead use his past to learn lessons that will help him make better choices today. By not wasting time dreaming about his future and ruminating about his past, Steve learns how to live in the present, which is the only way he is able to make effective changes in his life.

Steve's internal dialogue plays a significant role in how he views the world. His ingrained and automatic habit of seeing the worst in people and situations interferes with his growing and learning. His practice of dismissing everyone and everything limits his ability to consider plans of action for his life. His being demeaning toward everyone he encounters reduces his ability to form constructive personal and professional relationships.

When Steve catches himself negating an opportunity before he considers its positive potential, it will be beneficial for him to change his internal dialogue. For example, if he finds himself saying, *That's stupid*, he might change his internal dialogue to say, *Wait a minute. What am I telling myself? I'm telling myself this opportunity has no benefit for me. What do I really want to be saying to myself? It's probably a good idea to consider this situation and see if there is any part of it that may benefit me. I'm going to try harder not to jump to negative conclusions.* Steve may then reflect on what a good job he has done thinking this through and changing his thoughts. In this instance, Steve is using the Five Rs to recognize, reflect, rephrase, replace, and reinforce to change his negative internal dialogue into positive internal dialogue.

Another example might be when Steve initially thinks his new boss is a "jerk" because he instructed Steve it is unacceptable for him to be late again. Steve will be better served to stop to consider the reason his boss is upset with him. Instead of immediately using his internal dialogue to call his boss inappropriate names, Steve might recognize his boss is merely enforcing a commitment Steve made when he took the job. His boss is not reprimanding him without a reason. It was Steve's being late to work that resulted in the reprimand. Instead of saying, *My boss is a jerk,* it will be more constructive for Steve to say something like, *Stop. My boss is right. I was late for work. If I* want *to keep this job, I'm going to focus on being on time.* Steve is using thought-stopping to reframe his internal dialogue. He is stopping the negative thought and is replacing it with something positive and supportive that does not deny reality. He is also recognizing a choice. He does not have to get up on time to comply with an expectation. He wants to keep his job, so he chooses to get up early enough to be at work on time.

Over time, as Steve works on removing the negativity from his internal dialogue, he may discover his thought processes are changing. He may realize not everyone is wrong and not all situations are bad. He may discover there are benefits from being positive toward others, and that being responsible provides opportunities for his life. By developing more positive thoughts, interactions, and experiences, Steve may discover something new within himself—self-confidence. The confidence he gains through his successes may contribute to his developing a positive relationship with himself. He may come to realize the world is not ganging up on him. He may learn from his past experiences so he does not repeat the same mistakes in the present. He may realize it was necessary for him to acquire skills that allow him to build the life he wants to live.

# Seasons Change

Ruth taps the alarm off like she always does. The bed, the room, and the house are all the same. The difference is there is no familiar weight on the other side of the bed. The familiar snoring and cough are gone. This is the first morning without Joseph. Ruth reaches over and there is no one there. She glances at the unrumpled blanket, sheets, and pillows on Joe's side of the bed.

Ruth gets up with a sigh and reaches for her robe. She shuffles off to start her morning. Lucy had offered to stay with her for a few days, but Ruth does not want her daughter's tears stirring up her own grief. She is going to have to press on without Joe. There is no reason it shouldn't be today. Ruth thinks, *I have to be strong to get through this.*

As Ruth pours her coffee, she realizes she has made too much. *Stupid Ruthie*, she tells herself. *Joe's not going to have his three cups. I guess I might as well throw out the cream since I won't be using it.* As she pours the cream down the sink, Ruth looks out the window at the spot where Joe collapsed. He had fallen, clutching his chest, in the shade of the apple tree they planted when they married. The tree was broad now, with gnarled branches bowing low under the weight of many apples. She wonders, *How can I make cider and applesauce this year?* Now she cannot imagine getting close to that tree.

Ruth sits at the kitchen table cradling her coffee. Its warmth feels good against her arthritic fingers. She does not reach for the heap of mail on the table. It will be stacked with sympathy cards, all those people expressing their grief to her. She has enough grief right now without reading about theirs, too. The messages will just be more reminders Joe is gone. In the pile will be bills, too. Bills Joe took care of—insurance premiums, utilities, taxes, medical bills, and doctors' bills. It never seems to end. Why is it all so darned complicated now? It used to be you just went to the doctor and he billed you and you paid it. Now, they charge you for every little thing separately, and half the time you never see the person charging you. It is so hard now. It is all so hard. She mutters, "How am I going to get through it without Joe? Where am I supposed to start?" It makes her numb. The clock on the wall steadily ticks in the quiet kitchen.

Ruth contemplates. Was she supposed to call Joe's life insurance agent, or would the agent call her? Who is his agent now? What about all of Joe's stuff? He never really said who would get what. Will Lucy, John, and Robbie fight over his books, tools, clothes, and motorcycle? She grumbles, "The last thing I need now is for the kids to start arguing over Joe's stuff."

The worries flood in. *How much is owed on the house? How much is left on the mortgage we took out to buy the cabin on the lake? Oh, the cabin! The kids will certainly fight over that. Should I sell it so they can't fight over it? I may have to sell it depending on how much is owed on the house. I can't lose this house...our house. No, I guess it's just my house now. How much does Joe have in his retirement fund? Am I going to have to get some kind of job to keep the lights on? I won't take money from the kids to keep the power on, even if they offer to help. It's a parent's job to provide for their kids, not the other way around.*

Ruth begins to apply the Four Principles. *Ruthie, you're not doing yourself any good fretting about all this at once. You're going to bury yourself.* The voice in her head is a combination of Daddy, Joseph, and herself back when she would comfort her girls. It seems kind of silly to spend her life getting and giving good advice and not use any of it herself. *Take care of yourself today. Rest, eat well, and get some fresh air...and avoid the phone. This is your first day on your own. It is not necessary to do anything today. The best thing to do is rest, regroup, and get your strength back. The first thing to do is get something healthy into your belly.*

As Ruthie heats up some of Lucy's delicious casserole, it occurs to her she has not really eaten since Joe died, with the exception of a nibble here and there. She wipes away a few tears as she hears the pop and sizzle in the microwave. Joe always loved Lucy's casserole. Joe wouldn't get to taste this one, but he would have been happy to know she would still get to eat them. She would savor it and remember the times Joe would tease her to get the recipe from Lucy, even though she had taught her daughter how to make it. After Ruth finishes eating and cleans up the kitchen, she calls Lucy to tell her she is taking the day for herself. She assures Lucy she is okay, that she is taking a little time for herself.

It is a beautiful morning. The heavy dew is evaporating as Ruth putters across the front lawn. Cold weather would be coming soon, but there is no sign of it today. The beaming sun feels warm and comforting on her skin. She revels in the complex notes of birds chirping as she shuffles along the path to the park. She loves the bright oranges and reds of the berry-laden bushes. She stops periodically to hold a pretty leaf to examine the colors. A young woman approaches her, straining to keep a pair of corgi puppies from tripping her. The woman apologizes when the puppies bound up at Ruth's shins. Ruth laughs and stoops down to pet them. It takes a bit of effort, but she manages to feel their soft fur and little slobbery kisses on her hands.

After saying her good-byes to the pups and the kind woman, Ruth sits on the bench under a large maple tree. She closes her eyes and takes some deep breaths, the air heavy with the scent of wet grass. She listens to the leaves rustle above her head in the light breeze. Shrieks of joy echo from the nearby playground. Somebody is playing a flute, but she is only able to hear a few occasional notes. At this moment, this all feels so good.

After some time being present with these experiences, Ruth thinks, *I should probably get back in case someone comes by to check on me.*

*No,* she reminds herself. *Today is about taking care of me. This is my day. I will stay here as long as I want. Maybe I will amble down to the pond to feed the koi fish.*

By the time Ruth makes it back to the house, she is tired. She gives herself permission to take a nap. She had always rousted Joe off the couch when she thought he was sleeping the afternoon away, but today she is going to be the one sprawled out in the living room. When she wakes up, the sun is surprisingly low and the house is uncomfortably quiet. She turns on the TV for noise and shuffles to the kitchen to make a salad. The heap of mail is still on the kitchen table. She reminds herself the pile will be looked at tomorrow. She returns to the living room to eat her salad and watch a rerun of an old favorite show. The kids were little when this show was on. So many years had gone by.

Ruth watches TV for a little while, but despite her nap she is soon ready to go to bed. As she flips off the light in the kitchen, the mail still waits for her. *Tomorrow*, she reminds herself. She will not worry about it now. It will only keep her up all night. As she lies in bed by herself, it feels too big and empty without Joe. She bunches up his pillows in a line against her. It gives her a little comforting pressure. She knows she will not always do this, but tonight she wants a little reassurance, and the pillows still smell like him. Tomorrow she will begin the process of living alone. Ruth directs her mind to remember her time in the park. She focuses on the adorable corgi puppies, the smell of the air, and the happy chirps of the birds. She was fortunate to have such a good day. Joe would have been proud of her. Joe would have...the corgis...think of their cute little noses, those big shining eyes.

The next morning at breakfast, Ruth makes a list of things to do. The list seems endless. Insurance bills, bank issues, hospital bills, funeral bills, Joe's will, thank-you notes to concerned friends and relatives, and, of course, sorting out who will get what of Joe's stuff.

*One step at a time,* Ruth tells herself. *It is not possible to do it all in one day. You don't eat a whole cake all at once. This will take time, and the kids and others have offered to help.* She writes numbers next to each task on the list to prioritize them. She also jots down the initials of the person she will ask to help her with that task. There are a lot of Ls for Lucy, but Lucy is just like her mother, always wanting to get things done as soon as possible. Lucy will want to help and feel happier doing so.

As the days turn into weeks and the weeks turn into months, the list dwindles to nothing. Some days are harder than others. Some days the house is too empty. As Ruth grows to accept living without Joe, she begins considering what she wants for herself. Fortunately, there is no pressure to get a job to keep the house. The kids agree to buy the lake cabin together, and Joe had saved more money than she thought. Although she is able to afford to pay the bills and it is not necessary to work, Ruth wants to feel productive. Joe liked her at home, and she felt happy taking care of him. Now, with no one to take care of, Ruth feels she still has a lot to offer. She begins volunteering at the library to help keep things in order and encourage young folks to learn to love reading as much as she does. Ruth gets a corgi. Joe had always insisted that as long as he was alive, they would never get a "damn dog." Joe was gone, and if she could not enjoy Joe's kisses, she would instead enjoy Max the corgi's kisses as he nestled into her lap.

The holidays are the hardest of all. Ruth's house had always been the gathering place for Thanksgiving and Christmas. Now, Joe's absence is glaring. Ruth thinks carefully about what she wants from the holidays. Every decoration would bring back floods of memories of her life with Joe. Yes, these memories are precious, but they are too fresh this year. She recognizes it will be better to let her treasured memories of the past rest for a while. She will be better off focusing on all the blessings she has right now, especially her children and her grandchildren. Ruth allows herself to accept Lucy's offer to host Thanksgiving. Ruth insists on coming a few days early to help Lucy prepare the feast. The offer to help is an excuse to get out of the house, so she is able to create new Thanksgiving memories and not be anchored in nostalgia of past gatherings. At Christmas, Ruth stays with her son, Robbie. It would not be fair to expect Lucy to host all the holidays. On Valentine's Day, Joe had always placed a rose on her pillow with a small heart-shaped box of expensive chocolates. This February, Ruth treats herself to some special chocolates and gets Max, her new valentine, special yummy treats.

As spring blossoms into summer, Ruth accepts she is building a life for herself without her beloved Joe. She misses him and wishes he was still with her, sharing her life and her experiences, but her life now goes on without him. She looks forward to her visits with her children and her grandchildren. She finds satisfaction in her work at the library, and she loves snuggling with Max.

The Four Principles assist Ruth to move through her grief. Initially, Ruth feels she should take care of everything immediately after Joe's death. Instead, she gives herself permission to self-nurture so she will be able to deal with the stress she faces. She fills her water pitcher for coping by consciously making choices to eat well, rest, enjoy naturally occurring phenomena, and exercise. She remains in the present, which keeps her from becoming overwhelmed by her grief and all the tasks associated with Joe's death. She prioritizes the tasks and uses the cake analogy to recognize it is not possible to complete all the tasks at once. She allows herself to accept help from others. She does not feel she should do it all herself. Ruth uses supportive and encouraging internal dialogue, redirecting herself to the present when she worries about the future or thinks about the past.

As time evolves, Ruth develops goals for herself that are appropriate for her life now, rather than trying to relive past goals she had with her husband. Some of her new goals might be the same or similar as past goals with Joe, but it will be important for her to consider what she wants for her life today. She does not allow herself to get bogged down in her past. She does not spend time reminiscing about the past to the detriment of doing things she wants to do now, such as volunteering at the library and getting a corgi. Looking at her goals offers Ruth opportunities that were not feasible with Joe. Joe wanted Ruth at home, but with him gone, she is free to volunteer at the library. Joe never wanted a dog, but now she enjoys the company of Max.

During the holidays, Ruth faces making choices she wants. Rather than getting caught up in the expectation that she always hosts Thanksgiving and Christmas, Ruth creates opportunities to celebrate the holidays differently because of the changes in her life resulting from Joe's death. She seeks to celebrate the holidays in a manner that best works for her now. She recognizes that memories of Joe during the holidays are especially painful and she will feel better if she approaches the holidays differently, so she is not inundated with constant reminders of him. Additionally, staying with her children and their families gives her a chance to move forward and make new traditions. On Valentine's Day, she keeps the tradition of enjoying something special by getting herself chocolates. Instead of Joe receiving her affection, she now gives it to her dog, Max.

Throughout this process, Ruth makes choices. Some of them are small, such as her choice to take a nap the day after the funeral. Some are life-changing, such as her choice to no longer host the holidays. These choices support an internal locus of control. Ruth's journey demonstrates that even in the most difficult circumstances we have opportunities to make choices for our lives.

## A Rich but Empty Life

Sara is wealthy. It is not necessary for her to work. Despite not working, her days are frantic. Each morning she dashes down to the athletic club to work out with her trainer. After the vigorous routine to keep her body toned, she speeds back home to dress and put on her face. She often only has a moment or two to make sure the help is doing what they are being paid to do.

Sara usually has just enough time to meet her friends at Venito for a salad. The food is unimportant. It is the first glass of wine that makes it worth the trip and gives her the incentive she needs to face the rest of her day. After lunch, there is only enough time for a quick shopping spree to choose a few outfits. When she tries on an outfit, she thrills at the thought of how jealous other women will be when they see her in it...and the hungry stares of men who will want to see her out of it. Her new boobs accentuate the magic her workouts and hunger make possible. With every outfit she tries on, she calculates how many heads will turn. Almost every outfit, no matter how tight-fitting, is an option. Not many of her friends could say the same thing.

After spending too little time in the shops, Sara rushes back up the hill to prepare for that evening's dinner and event. There is always a fundraiser, party, play, or concert to attend. Her husband, Gene, likes the fundraisers the most. He wants her to be involved in as many charities as possible because they bring him into contact with so many potential clients.

Tonight is a typical evening. Sara waits for Gene to get home from work. They spent so much money renovating the house, but they never seem to spend any time here together. Gene, as usual, is later than he said he would be, but it is just as well. The longer he takes, the less time they will have to spend chuckling to inane banter with guests, while her feet ache in her amazing shoes. As she waits, Sara looks online for the right curtain and upholstery fabrics for the Colorado ski chalet.

As Sara drains another glass of chardonnay, she knows she has to keep her mind busy. She has to be looking at, planning for, or buying something. When she stops, the emptiness creeps in. The loneliness grows. The emptiness and loneliness always threaten to overwhelm her. It doesn't make sense. She has every-thing she ever dreamed of—the newest car, the best fashions, a big house with a pool. Everyone looks at her with desire and envy. And yet, she is not happy. She ponders what will make her happy. Her unhappiness seems to be growing. No amount of chardonnay, shopping, and events keeps the emptiness at bay. Something has to change, but she does not know what.

Sara looks at the glass of wine in her hand and thinks not drinking for a while might be a good place to start. Maybe she will be able to see things more clearly and figure out what she wants if her head isn't fuzzy from wine all the time. She recognizes that with almost everything she does and everyone she meets, she has a glass in her hand. Because she is able to see this about herself, she tells herself she does not have a problem with drinking. She thinks that without a drinking problem, it should be no problem to stop. If she doesn't drink, she won't have to work out so hard to burn off all those wine calories. She decides on three weeks without drinking. A whole month seems too long to not have any fun. Three weeks might work. It will be hard, but she can do it.

If she stays in town with her stocked fridge, her daily lunches of wine and salad with her friends, and all the evening fundraisers, she will never make it through three hours, much less three weeks, without a glass of wine. Sara talks to Gene who is supportive of her taking three weeks in Colorado. Sara buys a plane ticket to Colorado. After she clicks on the purchase icon and puts her phone down, she instinctively sips from her glass. *No!* she thinks. *This must stop. This is going to be the last drink.* After pouring the rest of her glass down the sink, she packs for her trip. She packs five bags of essentials and then realizes the winter help will not be at the chalet to lug them in for her. She is unable to decide what not to take. She is quitting drinking, not quitting living. She will just have to find someone to help her when she gets there. With her good looks, she knows she can always count on the kindness of strangers.

Sara barely makes her early-morning flight. Running a few red lights gets her to the airport in the nick of time. Colorado looks unfamiliar in the summer without its white coating of snow. As she expected, she is able to convince a passing jogger to haul her luggage into the chalet. After unpacking and scowling at the furnishings that so desperately need to be updated, she is uncertain what to do next. She has to find something to occupy her time that doesn't call for a glass of wine. Because sitting by herself at lunch would be uncomfortable and there would be plenty of wine within easy reach, she decides to pick up a salad and eat it on a bench at a walking trail. After eating, Sara thinks maybe this sobriety thing can be an adventure. She decides to take a walk in the woods. After only a few yards along the trail, fear of mountain lions compels her to scurry back to her car. She will find something to do that doesn't risk her getting eaten.

Sara speeds back into town to check out the shops. This time, she does not spend most of her time in the clothing stores. Instead, she spends time in the art galleries. She wants to buy some of the paintings, but she can't decide which ones will go best with her yet-to-be-determined furnishings. Her thoughts are constantly disrupted by urges to have a glass of wine. Her desire for chardonnay is so strong it muddles her thoughts and interferes with her ability to make a single purchase. That evening is miserable. Everything she thinks of for dinner would taste better with wine. She decides to go to bed instead of eating. She thinks the best way to avoid her cravings for wine will be to sleep through them.

After a fitful night, Sara wakes at dawn. She never gets up this early except to catch a flight. Yet, it seems strangely welcome—the early morning sun, birds chirping, and crisp air. She feels the urge to capture this experience somehow. She thinks of the paintings she perused in the galleries. Some of them weren't that good, yet they had price tags in the thousands. She has an idea. She will get brushes, paint, and canvases. She enjoyed drawing and painting as a girl. Maybe she will still enjoy painting. She will try it.

In solitude, Sara spends the next three weeks experimenting with painting the mountains, trees, and streams. She finds peace she has not felt for a long time, if ever. She does not miss work-outs with her trainer, lunches with friends, and uncomfortable shoes worn for hours at fundraisers. Sara is most surprised to discover she does not miss drinking wine. Her mind is clearer, and she enjoys waking up early when the sun has not yet cleared the mountains.

Let us take a look at Sara's life transition from the perspective of the Four Principles. She is learning how to nurture herself. By no longer drinking alcohol, she is creating a healthier environment for herself, and she is engaging in activities like painting that provide her with feelings of satisfaction. Until now, Sara has been using alcohol to nurture herself and cope with getting through her day. Alcohol has been an external locus of control. The external locus of control is dangerous for Sara, as her drinking may control her and develop into a habit in her attempt to cope with stress. It would benefit Sara to stop drinking altogether if she drinks as a means for coping and instead develop healthier coping strategies.

Sara has been living with a pronounced external locus of control. She has been living according to what she perceives she should do and what she thinks looks good to others. She is left vulnerable about how she feels toward herself, because she relies on others to validate her. This adds to Sara's feelings of emptiness. She is constantly looking outside herself for approval.

Before she travels to Colorado, Sara does things not because she wants to, but because they are a means to an end. Her workouts are not done for her health, but to keep her body appealing to others. The clothing she buys is not for comfort or function, but for how it impresses or entices others. Her charity work is not done out of a commitment to her beliefs or values, but to assist her husband in securing new clients.

It is time for Sara to look within herself to determine what she wants for her life. It is possible some of the things she should do are also what she wants to do, but it is important for her to take time to recognize what she truly wants to shift her perspective from an external to an internal locus of control.

Exercising is a positive nurturing activity. It will be better for Sara to approach her workouts from the standpoint of exercising for her health, rather than viewing it as a chore to keep her body acceptably trim according to her expectations of what beauty should be. Sara has allowed a societal expectation of a slim body and large chest, or "perfect figure," to dictate what she should look like to feel acceptable to others.

While shopping for clothing is a necessity, it will be better for Sara to shop according to what she likes, what feels comfortable, and what works best for her rather than basing clothing choices on what will impress others. As she focuses on selecting outfits according to what she likes, she may feel a greater sense of personal empowerment through individual expression.

Sara will benefit from supporting charities she finds most meaningful, rather than becoming involved merely to increase her husband's list of clients. By supporting charities she cares about, she is likely to find meaning and personal worth in her charitable efforts. By making a difference in causes she cares about, Sara will feel more effective and gain a greater sense of satisfaction.

By shifting from an external to an internal locus of control, Sara will make choices based on what works best for her and what she wants. She may find her workouts are similar to past workouts. Her clothes may be similar to her past wardrobe, and the charities she chooses to support may be the same or similar to the charities she supported in the past. The difference, however, is she will be making her choices based on what she wants and what fits for her, rather than complying with outside expectations. While the shift from external to internal locus of control is subtle, by determining what she wants through the choices she makes, Sara's sense of identity may become clearer. She is likely to feel less lonely and empty.

Sara will benefit from setting goals for herself. Goals will help Sara define where she wants to invest her time and energy today to make her future what she wants it to be. Achieved goals, big and small, will create feelings of accomplishment and confidence. They will provide Sarah with momentum to continue making positive choices in her life.

In the event Sara is unable to alter her alcohol use and continues to use drinking wine as a means for coping, it will benefit her to seek professional assistance, as she may be struggling with an addiction. If she realizes alcohol is the primary way she copes with life stressors, alcohol use is going to thwart her efforts to make positive changes in her life. Alcohol will be an ever-present external locus of control during her attempt to construct a stronger internal locus of control.

# Flooded with Guilt

Once Randy graduated from high school, he was done with books. He preferred to work with his hands, so he learned heavy equipment repair at a tech school. As the years passed, Randy created a simple but comfortable life with his wife, Louise, and their three children. Life was good as long as his hands could still turn a wrench and tie flies for fishing in the river next to their home.

The only part that wasn't good was all the traveling he did. Combines, bulldozers, and excavators were usually repaired wherever they broke down. It seemed Randy spent half his life pounding over empty dirt roads. How many suppers had he missed because he was fixing one stubborn piece of equipment after another?

One summer afternoon, Randy sets off to fix a broken combine at a farm. A storm is brewing, but Randy has gear with him for any weather. Rain soon hammers his truck, turning the washboard road into a slimy mess. The hill up to the farm would likely scare most folks, but Randy hoots in fun as he purposefully swings out the rear of the truck as it struggles to find traction. When Randy meets the farmer on his front porch, the farmer apologizes for bringing him out in such weather. Randy tells him it doesn't matter to him—bad weather is just part of the job. Luckily, the combine repair is not too bad, just a few sheared bolts Randy quickly removes and replaces. Once the rain stops and the fields dry, the old beast will be ready to chew crops again.

Randy has the farmer sign his soggy invoices, then roars down the hill. With this being the last job of the day, Randy hopes he can make it home for supper. Maybe he can take a hot shower and drink a beer or two before they all sit down to eat. There aren't many days he can do that.

On his way home, the road grows worse, but Randy grew up on muddy roads. He instinctively knows when to gun it and when to ease off. Randy sees a harmless-looking patch of flowing water covering the road ahead. Without hesitating, Randy floors it. The truck lurches hard to the right and there is no time to react as the truck rolls over and down into a ditch.

The next thing Randy remembers is waking up in the hospital. He tries to lift his arms, but they won't move. He is barely able to tilt his head because of the pain in his neck. From the corner of his eye he sees his right arm plastered in a cast. He glances over at his left arm, but he is unable to see it under the sheet covering him.

Once it is discovered Randy is conscious, his doctor gives him devastating news. Over a dozen people were swept away in a flash flood. Among the victims were Louise and his children. Their home had been swept off its foundation and splintered against the concrete bridge downstream. Randy is told he was fortunate to have survived. He almost drowned in the river he crashed into. He is told his injuries are severe, and they were unable to save his left arm, which had to be amputated above the elbow. With time, it is expected he will make a full recovery.

Randy clenches his eyes shut. His whole world and his whole life are gone. His wife, his kids, his home, and his left arm were gone in an instant. Randy's mind races, *How is this possible? What do I have left? What can I do? What is the point of living? I don't want to live like this. How can I live without Louise and the kids? It would just be easier to die.*

Let us consider how Randy may cope with this tragedy. Randy faces an extreme set of challenges. Because of the severity of his situation, Randy will benefit from extensive therapy and therapeutic support. He may also benefit from medication to treat depression and anxiety, as determined by his medical professionals. The period immediately following this trauma will be extremely difficult for Randy. As he moves through the initial shock of his circumstances, he faces deciding to live his life or succumb to grief. If Randy chooses to rebuild his life, recovery may take years of committed effort. Randy faces redefining his identity, what he finds satisfying in life, and how to live.

Given the Four Principles, take a moment to consider how Randy might move through his challenges and build a new life. Application of the Principles has been presented in several ways throughout this book. Hopefully, you are becoming familiar with how to implement them in different situations. While Randy's situation is extreme, the Principles still apply to the many challenges he faces.

First of all, and most importantly, it is for Randy to consciously recognize the importance of self-nurturing. If he does not fill his water pitcher for coping, his ability to address and overcome his many challenges will be diminished. If he does not take care of himself, he will not have the energy to cope with the significant losses in his life, physical rehabilitation, and psychotherapy. He faces the necessity of learning adaptive skills for working with one arm, career retraining, and any number of other challenges. This process of redefining his identity will consume a huge amount of water from his reservoir for coping. It will be important for him to place himself on a regular sleep-wake cycle, eat well, exercise regularly, and discover different nurturing activities. Randy will benefit from consciously taking time to appreciate all the things he is still able to enjoy and finds pleasurable. These may be as simple as enjoying the scent of the blossoms on the trees or the colors of a sunset. Some activities, such as fishing, may be more difficult to perform, but if they are done his way and he works with himself, they may still be rewarding and pleasurable.

It is crucial for Randy to stay present. If he lives in the past, it will promote depression. Given that so much of what Randy's life consisted of is now gone, it will be especially important for him not to compare what he had in the past with what he has today. Comparisons of the present to the past frequently result in negative internal dialogue, promoting feelings of inadequacy. For Randy, these negative thoughts may include being unable to do all the things he was able to do in the past. If Randy is telling himself he was better in the past than he is now, he may use thought-stopping to reframe the negative message. He may tell himself, *Stop. I'm learning how to do things differently given where I am now. I may not be able to do things like I used to, but I am learning how to do them my way now.*

If Randy stays in the past, he may become overwhelmed with all he has lost. He may be unable to move forward because of the weight of his grief. Randy will likely make many comparisons to how he had a family—a wife and three children—and now he is alone. If Randy's grief prevents him from completing tasks, even simple ones such as getting up in the morning or taking a shower, he may benefit from using his internal dialogue to redirect his thoughts. If he sets aside times for grieving, such as in therapy, a quiet moment, or at his family's gravesite, he may renew his focus on the task at hand and move forward in building his life.

If Randy worries about the future, it will create anxiety about all of the changes occurring in his life and the many difficult decisions he faces. He may feel overwhelmed and worry about how he will be able to function or earn a living after losing his arm. If he is unable to continue being a mechanic, it may be necessary for him to engage in training to develop a new career. These significant changes may initially appear overwhelming. However, by focusing on one thing at a time, completing one task at a time, Randy will make positive steps in rebuilding his life. Just as it is impossible to stuff an entire cake in our mouths, it will be impossible for Randy to instantaneously rebuild his life. However, if we eat one slice at a time, we are able to eat the whole cake. If Randy approaches his challenges one at a time, one task at a time, he will be more effective in moving his life forward.

In facing the sudden challenge of living without his family, Randy may be consumed with guilt over his perceived role in their deaths. He may regret his decision to live so close to the river that took his family. He may feel responsible for their deaths because he had been away working rather than being there to protect them when they needed him most. He may blame himself for driving carelessly and not getting a chance to save them. He may feel guilty just being alive when everyone he loves is not. All these thoughts are examples of tornado analogy thinking. Randy made the best decisions he knew how with the information he had at the time; his decisions were made with the best intentions. These decisions included living near the river, taking a job that demanded frequent travel, and hurrying home. There is no way for Randy to go back and change these decisions. His past has happened, and the only avenue open to him now is learning from his experiences and using that information when he makes choices today.

Randy may burden himself with negative internal dialogue. He may accuse himself of not being much of a man or a father because he has lost his entire family. He might call himself "selfish" for thinking more about the beers he looked forward to when he got home rather than being careful about making it there safely. He may tell himself he is worthless because he does not have two hands—that he is not good at anything besides being a mechanic. It will be important for Randy to transform his negative internal dialogue to positive internal dialogue that is supportive and does not deny his reality.

Randy is confronted with a sudden change in his identity. The loss of his dominant hand may lead him to struggle with completing simple tasks and force him to find a new way of earning a living. He may feel self-conscious over the loss of his arm. He may worry women will not find him attractive, or that it will be unlikely for him to ever have a family again, even if he wanted one. Randy's feelings of inadequacy may stem from expectations of what he thinks a man should be. To be effective, it will be necessary for Randy to meet himself where he is today. It will be beneficial for Randy to put his energy into recognizing things he is able and capable of learning to do, rather than lamenting what he is now incapable of doing. Instead of trying to be who he was in the past, Randy will be more effective when he recognizes who he is today. After this traumatic event, Randy is not less of a man, but a different man.

Randy faces challenges on a variety of levels in rebuilding his life. His situation is complex and multi-dimensional. At every step of his recovery, Randy faces making choices that build his life today for what he wants for his tomorrow...or he may remain focused on the past, which will not promote change for his life. He may choose to take care of himself, or he may choose not to. He may choose to be positive in his internal dialogue, or he may choose to be negative and critical. He may choose to learn ways to most effectively cope with having only one arm, or he may avoid physical and occupational therapy. He may choose to openly explore his grief in therapy, or he may attempt to deal with it on his own. Everything Randy faces is a choice. Some days will be easier than others. Some days may seem impossible and virtually pointless. However, if Randy openly evaluates what he is thinking and feeling, and if he applies the Four Principles when facing each challenge, he will likely increase his life satisfaction.

# Final Thoughts

While you were reading the above scenarios, some of them may have appeared extreme and unrealistic. However, difficult and unexpected life events may happen to any of us at any time. Hopefully, some of the scenarios triggered an awareness of similarities in your own life story. Whether the challenges we face are large or small, life-shattering or fairly inconsequential, we may all benefit from applying the Four Principles to improve our life satisfaction. Initially, it takes effort to apply the Four Principles, but with consistent practice their use will become easier and their benefits apparent.

Principle I: Self-nurturing and taking care of myself

Principle II: Learning to live in the present

Principle III: Developing a positive relationship with myself

Principle IV: Understanding and recognizing choices in life

I encourage you to learn and apply one principal at a time. Learn one, then incorporate the next principle, and so on. Start with learning how to nurture yourself, then move on to learning to live in the present while still nurturing yourself. Once you are able to stay present and nurture yourself, learn how to develop a positive relationship with yourself. After you have developed a positive relationship with yourself, start practicing the use of choice phrases to recognize choices in life. Approaching the principles in this manner allows one principle to build upon the other. The ultimate goal is to gradually incorporate them all into your life.

Developing and implementing the Four Principles will change the way you see the world. This change is a continual process. It is important to find your own way to apply and use them. The more you use them, the better you will become at discovering how you may apply them to your life. Initially, applying the Four Principles will require conscious effort, but over time and with consistent practice, they will become more natural and require less effort.

Learning the Four Principles is not something you do once and then are done. As you move through life, the challenges you face will change and evolve. Your use of the Four Principles will also evolve with your changing life circumstances. Because life always changes, it will be important to periodically evaluate how you are doing with your use of each principle. Ask yourself the following questions:

- Am I eating a healthy diet, regularly exercising, and consistently getting enough sleep?
- Am I taking time to have fun and play?
- Do I appreciate the simple pleasures in life?
- Am I living in the present, the past, or the future?
- What may I do today to make my tomorrow what I want it to be?
- Am I addressing one thing at a time?
- What have I learned from my experiences that I may use today?
- Am I placing my present reality onto the past?
- Did I make the best choices for my life in the past based on the information I had at the time?
- Is my internal dialogue kind and supportive, taking my reality into consideration?
- Am I recognizing and exercising my choices in life?
- Am I living life, or is life living me?

As stated earlier, this book is not intended to be a substitute for therapy with a mental health professional. If you diligently use the Four Principles and still find yourself struggling to overcome life's challenges, I encourage you to consult with a mental health professional. There are life circumstances that are much more effectively faced with the guidance of a mental health professional. Seeking assistance is not a sign of failure. Instead, it may be perceived as a constructive choice toward self-care.

The use of the Four Principles results in a conscious lifestyle. You will be consciously aware of how you eat, exercise, and sleep; how effective you are in the present; how you relate to yourself; how you think about yourself; and how you make choices in your life. You will also become consciously aware of the negative ramifications of unhealthy choices.

How you live life is a choice. If you consistently engage in choices that are positive, you will be more likely to experience life satisfaction. Conversely, if you consistently engage in choices that are negative, you will be less likely to experience life satisfaction. Ultimately, the choice is yours. It is up to you to determine how you want to live your life.

# APPENDIX A

# The Existential Psychodynamic Theory

In 1980, Dr. Irvin Yalom, a Professor of Psychiatry at Stanford University School of Medicine, wrote about his theory of existential psychodynamics, which explains how anxiety produced from existential concerns is processed by individuals in an attempt to cope with life. In his renowned book, *Existential Psychotherapy* (1980), Dr. Yalom proposes that personal dilemmas about our existence create anxiety. We face these personal dilemmas every day. He explains we each face resolving four specific internal challenges he identifies as "givens of existence," which he refers to as "ultimate concerns" (Yalom, 1980, p. 8) in life. These challenges are: coming to some understanding and resolution about our own death (death anxiety), seeking to find meaning in life, the desire to feel connected to others so we do not feel isolated and alone, and recognizing we have the freedom and choice to live our lives productively or unproductively. The most challenging "ultimate concern" to face and that creates the most anxiety is to address the reality we will not live forever. Dr. Yalom's premise is the more individuals face the reality of these "ultimate concerns" and come to terms with or find greater resolution for each of them, the more life satisfaction those individuals will experience.

# Defense Mechanisms for Coping

Dr. Yalom presents that there are three primary defense mechanisms to cope with the anxiety produced from confronting the "ultimate concerns." The defense mechanisms that allow us to feel safe and secure are repression, specialness, and ultimate rescuer. Repression is used to defend against all forms of anxiety. Specialness and ultimate rescuer defenses, however, are used only to defend against death anxiety.

The repression defense is when individuals try to push stressors—the things that cause stress—out of their minds. Repression pushes anxiety-provoking memories, thoughts, and ideas out of their awareness. By using repression, individuals may know something is wrong, yet they deliberately seek to ignore it.

The "specialness" defense (Yalom, 1980, p. 117) is when individuals believe they are so special they are not affected by the "ultimate concerns," so they do not find it necessary to process them. An example of this, identified by Dr. Yalom, is the fear and anxiety of aging. He describes that society strongly focuses on youth, and that those who dread aging may try to control their fear of death by attempting to remain youthful through dress and activities more suitable for younger people. He presents that individuals who use this defense tend to be self-sufficient, very independent, and unwilling to comply with recommendations or suggestions given to them from health professionals. This style of coping is reinforced through what Dr. Yalom calls "heroic individualism" (Yalom, 1980, p. 121), in which individuals recognize they will die. They attempt to "overcompensate" for lack of control over death through accumulation of prestige. Heroic individuals exhibit their specialness through achievements, awards, attaining material possessions or wealth, or through establishing monuments or estates that may be seen as reminders of their specialness following their death. The specialness defense may become compulsive as individuals work harder to push the reality of death out of their awareness (Yalom, 1980).

The "ultimate rescuer" defense (Yalom, 1980, p. 129) is when individuals believe someone else will shield them or take them away from the reality of the inevitability of their death. Here, individuals believe somebody, something, or some higher power will keep them safe from the "ultimate concerns." Dr. Yalom explains that individuals using the ultimate rescuer defense trust physicians, with all their knowledge, technology, and medicine, will be able to "cure" them of any and all ailments. This, obviously, is not a reality-based perception, but this belief provides comfort against potentially life-threatening illnesses.

Dr. Yalom describes that individuals who use the ultimate rescuer defense experience close, intense relationships and take care of the rescuer by giving them gifts or completing tasks for them. Doing this validates their existence. He states that individuals using this mode of defense will find ways to reinforce beliefs that someone or something will protect and care for them. While individuals may be lonely, they may not interact with others to confirm their belief in the ultimate rescuer. Isolation allows them to avoid exposure to contrary information that may dispel their belief in the ultimate rescuer. Dr. Yalom presents that the ultimate rescuer defense is not as effective at shielding oneself from the "ultimate concerns" as the specialness defense because it involves loss of personal identity (i.e., waiting for someone else to take care of me as compared to taking care of myself) (Yalom, 1980).

There is not a way to measure the specialness and ultimate rescuer defenses presented by Dr. Yalom. However, he identifies the concept of "locus of control" in psychological literature as analogous to the defenses of specialness and ultimate rescuer (Yalom, 1980, p. 157).

# APPENDIX B

---

# Testing the Theory

$D$r. Irvin Yalom's existential psychodynamic theory presented in his book *Existential Psychotherapy* (1980) inspired me during my doctoral training to empirically test one aspect of his theory. My dissertation, *Death Anxiety, Defensive Styles, and Life Satisfaction* (1994), focused on the relationships between the "given of existence" of death anxiety, reports of physical and psychological distress, and life satisfaction. A general summary of my research findings follows, and readers are encouraged to examine my dissertation for further details and explanations related to the findings.

## What is Death Anxiety?

The concept of death anxiety is complex and involves a great number of factors. For the purpose of this summary, a simplified definition of death anxiety is it comes from the tension arising from the conflict between our recognition we will die and the desire to continue living forever. Conscious death anxiety may manifest itself in different ways, including worrying about the act of dying, regretting unfinished projects, mourning the end of personal experience, or considering death rationally and dispassionately (Yalom, 1980).

Appendix A explains the concepts of the specialness and ultimate rescuer defenses and their analogous constructs of internal locus of control and external locus of control proposed by Yalom (1980). Readers are encouraged to read Appendix A to gain an understanding of these concepts and their role in defending against existential psychodynamics, which explains how anxiety produced from existential concerns is processed by individuals in an attempt to cope with life.

# Death Anxiety and Life Experience with Death

A relationship was not found between levels of death anxiety and life experience with death. Life experience was defined as encountering a situation in which an individual thought they were going to die and/or someone very close to them died. Those individuals who had life experience with death did not report having greater death anxiety than those who did not have life experience with death.

# Death Anxiety and Locus of Control

The prediction that death anxiety would be associated with both an internal locus of control and an external locus of control was only partially supported. An external locus of control (ultimate rescuer defense) was associated with higher levels of death anxiety, but an internal locus of control (specialness defense) was not associated with higher levels of death anxiety. Thus, higher levels of death anxiety were associated with the ultimate rescuer defense.

# Death Anxiety and Symptoms of Psychological and Physical Distress

A positive relationship was found between levels of death anxiety and symptoms of psychological and physical distress. In other words, if an individual has high death anxiety, that person is more likely to also be experiencing psychological and physical distress.

# Death Anxiety, External Locus of Control, and Symptoms of Psychological and Physical Distress

The defense of ultimate rescuer (external locus of control) to address coping with death was associated with reported symptoms of psychological and physical distress. However, a relationship was not found between death anxiety, the defense of specialness (internal locus of control), and reported symptoms of psychological and physical distress. In other words, if an individual uses the specialness defense to address death anxiety, this defense was not associated with reports of psychological and physical distress. Results revealed individuals with high death anxiety were extremely controlled, perceived death as powerful, and events as resulting by chance. Individuals with less death anxiety, however, with more internal locus of control, saw others as less powerful and did not attribute happenings to chance. High death anxiety was found to be associated with an external locus of control (ultimate rescuer defense), but it was not found to be associated with an internal locus of control (specialness defense).

# Level of Repression and Psychological and Physical Distress

A relationship was found between levels of repression and reported symptoms of psychological and physical distress. In other words, if an individual was not able to push stressors out of their consciousness, they reported greater levels of psychological and physical distress.

# Death Anxiety and Repression

A relationship was found between death anxiety and repression. Individuals reporting higher levels of death anxiety also have higher levels of repression. Similarly, those reporting lower levels of death anxiety reported less repression. These findings support the idea that death anxiety at low levels may be approached, talked about, and perhaps even explored with an individual. However, as the level of death anxiety increases the ability to approach the anxiety is decreased, as the anxiety becomes more threatening and the individual must defend against it. Levels of death anxiety may fluctuate due to circumstances and life stress.

# Locus of Control and Reported Symptoms of Psychological and Physical Distress

The prediction that an internal locus of control and an external locus of control would be associated with reports of psychological and physical distress held up only for an external locus of control, not for an internal locus of control. Individuals who have an external locus of control reported experiencing greater psychological and physical distress. Individuals who have an internal locus of control did not report experiencing greater levels of psychological and physical distress. Thus, it appears the defense of specialness is more effective than the defense of ultimate rescuer in coping with life stressors.

# Death Anxiety and Life Satisfaction

A relationship was found between how well a person copes with the reality of their own vulnerability in life (death anxiety) and how satisfied they are in life (life satisfaction). Acknowledging mortality and confronting death anxiety resulted in feelings of greater life satisfaction. That is, individuals who reported being satisfied with life—who felt good physically and emotionally, were optimistic about the future, were flexible, and welcomed change and variety—reported less death anxiety.

# Internal Locus of Control and Life Satisfaction

An inverse relationship was found between internal locus of control (specialness defense) and life satisfaction. Those individuals who look within themselves typically experience greater life satisfaction than those who look outside themselves for answers.

# REFERENCES

---

Godley, C.S. (1994). *Death anxiety, defensive styles, and life satisfaction*. Unpublished doctoral dissertation. Colorado State University.

Godley, C.A. & Gillard, M.A. (2011). "Assisting handlers following attacks on dog guides: Implications for dog guide teams." *Journal of Visual Impairment & Blindness, 105*(10), 601-611.

Yalom, I.D. (1980). *Existential psychotherapy.* New York: Basic Books.

REFERENCES

# SUGGESTED READING

Altman, D. (2011). *One minute mindfulness: 50 simple ways to find peace, clarity, and new possibilities in a stressed-out world.* Novato, CA: New World Library.

Covey, S. (2014). *The 7 habits of highly effective people: Powerful lessons in personal change.* New York: Simon & Schuster.

Lyubomirsky, S. (2007). *The how of happiness: A scientific approach to getting the life you want.* New York: Penguin.

Peck, S. (2003). *The road less traveled: A new psychology of love, traditional values and spiritual growth.* New York: Simon & Schuster.

Seligman, M.E.P. (2006). *Learned optimism: How to change your mind and your life.* New York: Vintage Books.

Tolle, E. (2004). *The power of now: A guide to spiritual enlightenment.* Novato, CA: New World Library.